To Maxine

Best Wishes

The story of a not-so-ordinary man who gave it up for more, a fascinating read from start to finish...a real insight to life as a player and to life as a Christian and what it means. An honest, sincere, and real thought-provoking book...you can only admire him for giving up all he had and wanting more... which Gavin will tell you he has found.

Robbie Fowler
Former Liverpool and England International Player

What a fabulous book! A must-read for all – not just football fans. I loved working with Gavin as his manager at Chelsea and I've always said he was in my top 3 players I ever signed as a manager. His talent has shone through again in this wonderful book. A beautiful insight to Gavin's life and an inspiration to all. Loved it!

Glenn Hoddle
Former England and Chelsea Manager

I've enjoyed knowing Gavin both as a footballer and co-commentator over many years. I'm full of admiration for him and the way he lives out his faith. I'm thrilled to see him thrive as a pastor in Canada and look forward to the release of his autobiography.

John Motson
Television and Radio Football Commentator

Gavin's story includes playing for some of the top managers in football including Harry Redknapp, Kevin Keegan, Ossie Ardiles and Glenn Hoddle. I played against Gavin a number of times and he was an outstanding professional but perhaps more importantly, he was also a man of very good character.

David Moyes
West Ham United Manager

Such a thought provoking read, especially when football can cocoon you into its own little material world, which at times does not seem to be in touch with reality.

Gavin through his faith was able to keep himself firmly focussed throughout his football and media career to his real true destiny.

It was a real pleasure to spend time with Gavin in the dressing room all those years ago

Les Ferdinand
QPR Director of Football
Former England, QPR, Spurs and Newcastle United Striker

This book is not your standard ex-professional footballer's autobiography. It's much more than, 'I played here, against this player at this stadium. This was the score, etc.' It contains much more. This story is a one-off! It is an insight into how Gavin dedicated himself from an early age to become a professional footballer; the gamble he takes to drop down the leagues to gain the experience and rise to play at the highest level.

It's a story of a very close family. It's a story of a top sportsman, then a successful television pundit, who then sacrifices financial security for his beliefs. Be prepared for an insight into the workings of some of the top football managers in England. Also be prepared for some thought-provoking, straightforward opinions on society today. I thoroughly recommend this read.

Alan Curbishley
Former Charlton Athletic and West Ham United Manager

To be successful in one career takes talent and determination. To do so in three careers is something else. Gavin Peacock's life story is unique. His autobiography is fascinating.

Lance Hardy
Author, TV Editor, Former Editor at BBC Sport

Pastor Gavin Peacock has written a must-read book. He takes readers on a fun, insightful and nostalgic journey through his life. *A Greater Glory* spoke to me personally. Reading through every page gave me more enlightenment as to how blessed I am to be alive in Christ doing the things I love to do. This book has all the elements of life in it and I would recommend it in a heartbeat.

Jonathan Mensah
Columbus Crew – MLS, Ghanaian International Footballer

This book is a very well written and fascinating account of a professional footballer's family life, with a great insight into how the industry works, its ups and downs, pressures and triumphs and disappointments.

But for me this book is about life itself, including religion, beliefs, and the sacrifices you have to make to have the life you want. It's about making vital decisions under pressure that not only affect you but your whole family. What's important in life for the individual is so different and complex! I thoroughly recommend this book!

Gerry Francis
Former Queens Park Rangers and Tottenham Hotspur Manager

Obviously, I know Gavin from our time we played together at Newcastle and our Charlton links, but this really is one of the most interesting and fascinating autobiographies I have read in a long time.

A successful footballer to BBC pundit to Christian Pastor!! Not many players have had such a diverse and fulfilling life.

Rob Lee
Former England and Newcastle United Footballer

A fascinating read about an alternative lifestyle path for a footballer. Gavin puts as much passion and focus into his life, as he did into his performances as a player. A great man on and off the pitch.

Pete Graves
Sky Sports Presenter

To enhance our Asia-wide broadcasts of the Premier League in the early 2000s, we developed a roster of visiting pundits who would come and spend a fortnight in Singapore appearing on various shows. When Gavin came to town, I already knew we were going to get a different kind of pundit – his thoughtful analysis and measured insights on British TV had already caught my eye. We clicked, on and off screen, and in the time we spent together, both working and socially, I soon realized his was an inquiring mind and nature – one that would not be satisfied by simply being part of the football media scene. Even so, the spiritual journey upon which he embarked surprised me at first. Upon reflection – and now that he has described that journey in these pages – it makes sense.

Gavin has a clear sense of who he is, where he has come from, and what he believes to be his purpose in life. How many of us can say that?

This is about as far as you could possibly get from your 'traditional' footballer's autobiography. Given the almost unprecedented journey upon which he has embarked, it is both essential and fascinating to learn what shaped Gavin, from his family to his career in football to his faith.

John Dykes
TV Presenter, Commentator, Event Host Fox Sports Asia, ESPN

I'm very honoured to be asked to forward a few words to this book. I was fortunate to be around at the start of Gavin's football journey. We met at England schoolboy trials and hit it off from then on. I've been blessed to know his family from a mere boy. This sports book takes you on a journey to the core of the man I can call a friend for life. It's got belief, laughter, honesty, and sorrow. The most powerful thing he got from his parents was integrity. It's a must-read for any sports enthusiast!

Michael Thomas
Former England, Arsenal and Liverpool footballer

What a phenomenal read! Gavin's life story (so far!) surely resonates with many, many people. A proud family man, a never-say-die attitude as a professional footballer and BBC presenter. Not forgetting of course, the assuredness in his mind, body and soul of his ultimate goal!

Alex McLeish
Former Scotland and Rangers Manager

The world is struggling with identity but the way Gavin articulates this in his book is truly inspirational. A man with purpose and destiny – who unashamedly has a love for his faith.

Michael Johnson
England U21 Coach. Former Birmingham and Derby Footballer

Unlike any footballer's autobiography you've ever read. Honest, intelligent and sincere. Rather like the man himself.

Tom Watt
Actor, Author, Broadcaster

I love reading biographies and autobiographies. Sporting and Political. I have read so many from Alex Ferguson to Andre Agassi, Margaret Thatcher to Tony Benn. But Gavin Peacock's *A Greater Glory* is one of the best I have ever read. It is superbly written, interesting, funny, littered with great anecdotes and thought-provoking. An all-round brilliant read.

Alun Ebenezer
Headmaster, Fulham Boys School

If you love sport, read this book. If you want to grasp the resilience required to be a professional footballer, read this book. If you would like to understand how Christianity and sport fit together, read this book. In short, read this book!

Graham Daniels
CEO, Christians in Sport

A Greater Glory is such a well-written book. Gavin's story is varied, gripping and moving. I've never before read such an evocative description of how it actually feels to score a goal at the top level. Nor have I read a more spine-tingling account of what it feels like to step up to the pulpit and preach. Football feels like a matter of life and death to some of us, but the gospel truly is…and Gavin gives us a pitch-side seat as we experience the wonder of both.

Football, like politics, can become an object of ultimate hope. It can feel all important, you can build your life around it, it can be exhilarating and there may be glories along the way…but those glories will not last. Gavin takes us on a journey that is genuinely thrilling, often really funny, sometimes deeply moving and in the end, simply inspiring.

Tim Farron
MP, Former Leader of the Liberal Democrats

This book is compelling, candid and clear. For those who love the beautiful game there is much here that will fascinate and inform you about what is involved in becoming and being a professional footballer. For those who are Christians there is much here to do the same and a whole lot more. Is it possible to be a professional footballer and a committed Christian? What is involved in making it to the top of the professional game as a Christian? What is there after the final whistle and your career is over? All of this and more is addressed by Gavin Peacock in this book.

Written with pathos, Gavin's humble assessment of himself and generous evaluation of others in the football world coupled with his growing conviction about the most important things in life will cause you to laugh, cry and think. I believe no one will read this book without benefit, I am delighted to commend it to you.

Robert Briggs
Pastor of Immanuel Baptist Church, Sacramento, CA;
President of Reformed Baptist Seminary, Sacramento, CA and
Chaplain of Sacramento Republic FC

Gavin was a superb footballer, but more importantly a wonderful guy. His life story will be one of the football best ever reads for sure.

Harry Harris
Author, Former Chief Football Writer for The Daily Mirror,
Two-time British Sports Journalist Of The Year

A fascinating insight into how one man coped with the vicissitudes of life in the world of football and beyond. From professional footballer to pundit to preacher is quite some journey. No Damascene moments, just a gradual and growing awareness of the power of faith, which is now central to his life. Despite being an agnostic I found his writing both moving and inspirational. A very good read.

Guillem Balague
Spanish Football Journalist, Author, Pundit

Reading Gavin's fascinating memoirs sent me down memory lane to our talks and discussions on nights before away matches. *A Greater Glory* simply confirms the impression that I got of a curious, self-reflecting, helpful, yet ambitious gentleman.

At a time when so many people get lost in the superficial world of social media, this book will provide simple tools for anyone to find purpose in life.

Jakob Kjeldbjerg
Danish TV Presenter. Former Chelsea FC Footballer

A special man's goal of finding his Holy Trinity, through a fascinating, thought-provoking journey of football, family and faith. A story for our time and all times.

Mark Saggers
TV Presenter and Talk Sport Radio Host

A pacey book filled with passion and purpose, the principles of the man and the power in his message shines through!

Kriss Akabusi OBE
Former Team GB Olympic Medalist

Gavin Peacock can't just score goals, he can write. So he tells you what it feels like to play in the FA Cup Final, to be on the pitch with Glenn Hoddle, to be managed by Kevin Keegan, Sir Bobby Robson and Ruud Gullit.

But alongside those stories, what I appreciated most in this book was a priceless wisdom that has enabled him to navigate life. So how do you work out relationships, disappointment, disability, parenting, marriage, career? In chapter after chapter I just loved the paragraphs that explained how he was thinking and anchored in Jesus Christ when he was confronted by life's complexity. There was gold in chapter after chapter. A riveting read that I thoroughly recommend to all.

Rico Tice
All Souls Church and Christianity Explored

Gavin Peacock is a unique guy who takes sport seriously and faith even more seriously. I've loved getting to know him over the past few years as he has great stories and yet still manages to inspire deeper more passionate faith. I'd recommend this book to anyone. Even if you don't share his faith. And even if you don't support Chelsea!

Keith Getty, OBE
Hymn Writer and Liverpool Fan

As a pastor who would have loved to be a footballer, I really enjoyed this book about a footballer who loves being a pastor. A rare combination of insight from one who has been embraced by the pulpit having excelled on the pitch. Few people are qualified to write such a book. Gavin Peacock is one of them and he has done a terrific job.

If you've ever wondered what goes on before 'the game' and after 'the sermon' this book is for you. A terrific story of someone who has spent his life heading towards the goal to receive a prize that doesn't tarnish with time.

Alistair Begg
Senior Pastor of Parkside Church, Cleveland, Ohio, and Broadcaster of Truth for Life ministry

A GREATER
GLORY
FROM PITCH TO PULPIT

GAVIN PEACOCK

CHRISTIAN
FOCUS

Copyright © Gavin Peacock 2021

hardback ISBN 978-1-5271-0679-6
epub ISBN 978-1-5271-0737-3
mobi ISBN 978-1-5271-0738-0

10 9 8 7 6 5 4 3 2 1

Published in 2021
reprinted in 2021
by
Christian Focus Publications Ltd,
Geanies House, Fearn, Ross-shire,
IV20 1TW, Great Britain.

www.christianfocus.com

Cover design by James Amour

Cover image: 'Original Wembley Stadium (1923)'
by Allen Galaviz Gerardo

Photo credits: back cover photo and 'A family portrait' (photo section) courtesy of Anna Michalska. Back interior flap photo and 'Preaching the Word' (photo section) courtesy of Jared Harfield.

Printed and bound by
Bell & Bain, Glasgow

CONTENTS

For my gentle and graceful wife, Amanda. My greatest helper and one true love. This story doesn't work without you.

It is the greatest privilege to be your husband.

Till death do us part.

'"Therefore a man shall leave his father and mother and hold fast to his wife, and the two shall become one flesh." This mystery is profound, and I am saying that it refers to Christ and the church.' (Eph. 5:31-32)

FOREWORD

A very significant proportion of children dream of becoming footballers but in reality only a tiny number ever get anywhere near a professional club. Further, for the highly talented handful who do join an elite club as schoolchildren, an equally small percentage ever achieve professional status. Finally, you may be surprised to read that the average duration of an adult football career in English football is six seasons. When I tell you that Gavin Peacock played over 600 games and scored over 130 goals in an 18-year career, you can begin to understand why his career was so impressive.

One of the reasons it is so difficult to stay in the game having actually achieved professional status, is that there is tremendous pressure to perform. This pressure is not limited to match days, in front of thousands of spectators in the stadium and millions on the television, it also applies to the way you are expected to conduct yourself in day-to-day interactions at a professional football club. Gavin declared he had become a Christian in 1986 at the age of eighteen, when he was a young professional at QPR – at the time one of the top teams in England. He might as well have jumped into the Lions' Den. There were hardly any Christians in professional football in the early 1980s and football club culture was completely unforgiving in its mockery of anyone who stepped out of line with institutional expectations. Gavin hardly gave this a second thought; indeed, quite the reverse since he was playing in the first team within a year, at the unusually young age of nineteen.

I met Gavin shortly before he joined Newcastle United in 1990. His ability to integrate Christian faith with a top-level football career was already outstanding. As team captain he led from the front on and off the field, with everyone at the club fully aware that he saw his vocation in football as a gift from God. At the age of twenty-three he was becoming a highly respected ambassador for Christ in professional football. After three very successful seasons in the North-East, Gavin moved back to London, leaving the management of one football legend Kevin Keegan to sign for another English footballing great, Glenn Hoddle, at Chelsea. More playing success followed under Gavin's captaincy, where he almost changed the course of the 1994 FA Cup Final when his terrific shot rattled the bar against Manchester United at Wembley.

It was in this period that Gavin became a significant influence on the growing number of Christians in English football. This was initiated when he and his wife Amanda began hosting a monthly Christians in Sport footballers' gathering in their home. Many attended over the course of the next decade, some who would not have said they were Christians, many younger players finding their feet in the profession, and a growing number of those who were developing a mature faith. The model initiated in the Peacock home was multiplied around the country. Throughout the 1990s and 2000s, similar monthly gatherings emerged in major cities across the UK as a result of Gavin's vision.

Gavin retired from football in 2002, at the age of thirty-five. It was no surprise that within a very short time he became recognized as an intelligent and articulate broadcaster on the two major football outlets, the BBC and Sky Sports. His six years in these roles were very successful and it was likely that his people and leadership skills would take him to the pinnacle of his new profession. When Gavin knew that it was time to leave the BBC to train to become a Christian pastor, he acted with typical decisiveness, set off for college training in the UK and then, in due course, to Canada. Make no mistake, he was turning his back on a second, stellar career by leaving broadcasting. Indeed, a broadcast on the BBC's *Football Focus* in 2008 was the only time in my life where I watched the Christian faith expressed clearly and in everyday vernacular as the centrepiece of a British, prime time sports programme.

Gavin has now established himself in the third aspect of his vocation as a leader of people. He leads by serving God's church as a Christian pastor. Meanwhile, he continues to be a faithful friend to those of us in the UK who continue the work of reaching the world of professional and competitive sport for Christ. Gavin served the cause well. On his watch as a Christian player and broadcaster over two decades, the influence of Christianity in English football advanced from a mere handful to many scores of players. Today, it is assumed by everyone in the game that there are Christian players and coaches at most professional football clubs. What has not been articulated is that many of those who now lead the cause of Christ as managers and coaches in English football were contemporaries of Gavin Peacock and saw what it looked like to be a Christian and a top player, both on and off the pitch. That has been his legacy to the world of professional football in England, for which many of us are extremely grateful.

This is a great read and I know you'll enjoy it. It is a different kind of sports biography. It's a story about life in all of its complexities: a story of family and faith, fame and fortune, of suffering and pain, of winning and losing and starting again, of love and loss, of where we find our true identity and the hope of glory.

Before signing off, can I make one plea? Keep looking beyond Gavin to the God who gave him his footballing, communication and leadership talents. Then you will properly understand both the man himself and the purpose of the book in your hands.

Graham Daniels
General Director, Christians in Sport
Director at Cambridge United Football Club

INTRODUCTION: TWELVE STONES

There is a man in the Bible called Joshua. He was Moses' successor. I love Joshua. He was a great captain: a leader and a mighty man of courage who led Israel across the River Jordan after God parted the waters, and into the Promised Land of Canaan. Interestingly, God then told Joshua to mark the occasion by collecting twelve stones and setting them as a memorial: the purpose of the memorial was that the people would remember God and tell their children about His sovereign, saving grace so that all people everywhere would know and trust the Lord.

I am fifty years old as I begin to write. Fifty is a milestone in life and so this book is a memorial of sorts; my twelve stones (in twelve chapters). As the name suggests, autobiographies are generally written by people about themselves. On one level you can read this book that way. It's my story: a memorial of the life of a boy from the south east of England in Kent, who lived a schoolboy dream as a professional footballer and went on to another dream career as a BBC commentator, but who gave it all up for church ministry; a story which takes you all the way from the pitch to the pulpit. But there is another way of reading this book: a way that underpins and overarches all of this. That is to read it as a memorial of God's sovereign, saving grace in a man and to see how knowing Jesus Christ as your Lord and Saviour is the most necessary thing in life. Because there is more to life than football, fame and fortune. There is a greater joy and a greater glory to be had. The key to happiness is found elsewhere, through faith in a carpenter from Nazareth – the most famous person in history – and His life, death and resurrection.

Is this a 'religious' book and do you need to be a Christian to read it? Not at all. But although this is a book about football, it also touches on some of the deep problems in our culture and the deepest issues of life, and points to where true hope and meaning are found. I hope you read it in the first way and enjoy it as an autobiographical memorial that's somewhat different from your regular 'ex-footballer turned football pundit' book – though everyone's story is surely valuable. However, my hope is that you also read it in the second way: as an autobiography that is actually about someone else: a memorial of God's grace. And that through this you would come to know and trust Him with me. Then these twelve stones will have served you well.

1

INCHES: THE FINE LINE BETWEEN VICTORY AND DEFEAT

Picture this. It's May 1994. The Wembley atmosphere is electric as rain falls on the pristine turf. A sea of Chelsea blue and Manchester red surrounds me, as 90,000 people cram into the world's greatest stadium to watch the world's greatest domestic cup final. They say it's every schoolboy's dream to play in an FA Cup Final and thousands of young kids around the world are watching amongst the 90 million global TV audience.

The scene is set. It's Chelsea *v.* Manchester United; Blues *v.* Reds; South *v.* North. Manchester United have already won the Premier League. I'm playing for Chelsea but United are the better team. Nevertheless, despite them being League Champions we have beaten them 1-0 twice this season, home and away. And I scored both times. This season, we are their bogey team and I am their nemesis.

All my senses are heightened as I walk onto the pitch; Hoddle, Wise, Spencer, Stein and Cascarino are next to me. It's as if I see everything in Technicolor, feel every drop of rain, spot individual friends and family members in the crowd. I glance up and see my wife, Amanda. As long as she is here everything's okay. I remember our new baby, Jake, not even a year old and safe at home with my wife's mother. I see my parents. Beaming.

They've followed me every step of the way. A thumbs up from my father. Mum by his side. That's all I need from them.

I look across at the opposition led out by their great Scottish manager, Alex Ferguson. They are simply outstanding. Their flying wingers Andrei Kanchelskis and young Ryan Giggs are irresistible on their day. Welshman, Mark Hughes, is physically too strong for most defences. He is paired in a striking role with the awesome, Eric Cantona. No one will grace the Premier League in the 1990s like 'King Eric'. The Frenchman has power, skill and unshakeable confidence in his ability to do the unusual and win matches. He's the best around. My team-mate, Eddie Newton, and I are up against a formidable midfield duo of Roy Keane and Paul Ince. Excellent passers of a football. Hard as nails. Fiercely competitive.

But they hold no fear for us. Our player-manager Glenn Hoddle has begun a transformation at Stamford Bridge – a revolution of sorts. He's changed our style from 'direct and muscular' to 'skilful and mobile'. He's changed our eating habits from tea and biscuits after training to pasta and salad. He's changed the Heathrow practice pitches from West London winter mud heaps with airplanes flying overhead to flat grassy surfaces...still airplanes flying overhead!

I am Hoddle's first signing at the beginning of the season – £1.25 million from Newcastle United. It's a significant fee. After briefly being bottom of the league at Christmas we have climbed back up to mid-table and had a tremendous cup run. I've scored in every round including two against Luton Town in the semifinals a few weeks earlier at Wembley: a result that puts Chelsea in their first FA Cup Final for twenty-four years. The fans have hope once more. We are a good cup team. We have the measure of United. The movement and interplay of our frontline with Stein (5' 6"), Spencer (5' 6"), Wise (5' 7") and me, fits Hoddle's new footballing style. I'm the tallest at 5' 9".

The Mighty Midgets they call us; and we're causing problems for the best of teams.

The build-up for an FA Cup final is more exhausting than the actual game. There are weeks of TV and newspaper interviews. Cameras around the training ground increase and intensify. The players appear at local children's charities, advertise the newest sets of golf clubs and record the obligatory cup final song! Family and friends want tickets for the match. Everyone is coming. The regular season finishes. The nation's focus is all on the final. The pressure mounts daily.

The morning of the match arrives. The team hotel. My Danish roommate, defender Jakob Kjeldberg, gets out of bed looking ready for war. Breakfast. Newspapers. A team walk. A team talk. Pre-match meal: chicken and pasta. I can barely eat as the nerves seem to focus on my stomach. Cup final suits. The coach to the stadium. Playing our favourite song as we look out the windows. Coming down Wembley Way and seeing the famous Twin Towers and the scene of so much history, not least where England won the World Cup in 1966. Fans are everywhere. Thousands of them. Cheering, running alongside the coach, faces painted blue. It means so much to them. Their hopes rest on us. More butterflies in the stomach: this is huge!

The dressing room. The baths are so big and deep you can literally dive into them. Out to inspect the pitch. Firm but wet. Medium length stud for me. Puma Kings – size 8. We head back inside. Envelopes with tickets for family and friends. Telegrams with good wishes. Shirts hanging. Love the blue! Number 10 – 'Peacock' on the back. 'FA Cup Final 1994' embroidered on the chest. Kiss the Chelsea badge. Can't let the fans down.

Coach, Graham Rix, says, 'Gavin, it will fly by. Enjoy the day!'

Now, Hoddle's final words: 'We can do this. Go make some history, boys!' I say a quick prayer – not to win but to honour

God win or lose. We make our way down the tunnel. They see us at the far end of the stadium first, as the plastic tunnel extends onto the pitch. The far end of Wembley begins to cheer. The roar wraps around us like a swirling wind as we walk into full view. Electricity through the body! Goosebumps on the neck. The national anthem. Presented to royalty. Break away. Get to position. Can't hear my team-mates. The noise is too much. This is it. I can't wait to start. Heart beats fast…feels like it's in my mouth…. Then in an instant my nerves are gone. Ice flows through my veins. Referee, David Ellery, blows the whistle. GO!

I get an early touch of the ball. An easy pass. We begin well. I feel good. Like I can run all day. My fitness is supreme. The game plan? Keep it tight in defence. Don't let Giggs and Kanchelskis get on the outside of us. Our fullbacks, Frank Sinclair and the experienced Steve Clarke, are doing a good job, man-marking them. Frank is lightning quick. Clarkey is our most consistent player – so reliable. We are breaking forward well. I'm finding space. Our forwards, Spencer and Stein, are getting chances. Cantona is quiet and United are on the back foot.

And then comes the moment. Twenty minutes into the game. I win a header against Paul Ince. (Always a good battle with him. We grew up playing against each other.) A loose clearance from United defender, Gary Pallister, and I anticipate it a fraction before Ince. I get my chest to the ball and knock it forwards. Just enough. It comes up quick off the wet pitch and back towards my body. Momentum is taking me forward. I must get another touch. Arms out for balance. A right foot flick. The ball's ahead of me now – ahead of Ince too. That's good. It's coming down on my left side. Not a problem.

***

'You've got to be able to use both feet, son. Learn it and your whole game will open up.' My dad's words from the time I could kick a ball ring in my ears. Right foot, left foot. Up against the wall in the garden, on the street, on the training field. Right foot, left foot. Different angles. Different techniques. Extra practice. Hour after hour after hour. All for one moment in a match.

***

I've been doing this since I was five. Practice becomes habit and habit becomes instinct when the pressure's on. All in one movement. Chest. Right foot. Now let fly with my left. Head down! I don't even feel the ball leave my foot. I know it's good…. And time stands still.

Everything slows down. The noise of the crowd fades in my ears as Peter Schmeichel, Manchester United's huge Danish international goalkeeper, begins to stretch for the ball. He's off his line! The shot is too good! It's dipping over him! It's in, I think. 1-0 to Chelsea. Peacock scores again! They'll think it's not their year. We'll have one hand on the cup! Schmeichel dives backwards. The big Dane stretches his long frame. The ball loops over him. Goal!!! No! Smack! It hits the crossbar. Everything returns to normal speed. They are on the counter-attack. We go in 0-0 at half time. We're playing well, but an inch lower and we would have been one up. If only….

***

Half-time intervals are a funny thing in football. Sometimes you can't wait for them to come. You need a rest. The opposition is hammering you and you need to regroup. But sometimes you don't want the first half to end. You're playing well. The opposition is under pressure. It's only a matter of time before you score. This is one of those times. I want to stay out there. We can smell blood. United are not on their game. We get into the dressing room. Buzzing.

'Brilliant lads. You're doing well', Hoddle shouts.

'Get some water down you', says Terry Byrne, the kit man.

'Any injuries? Anyone?' asks Bob Ward, the physio.

I briefly wonder what is happening in the United dressing room. I think they'll be a different team in the second half.

Hoddle again, 'They'll come at you boys. Don't do anything silly in the first twenty minutes. Hold fast. You'll get more chances. We can nick it.'

The buzzer goes. Out we go. The rain is relentless and Manchester United are coming at us now. I feel the difference. Momentum is a strange thing. One minute you seem to have it and the next it's gone. But it is vital in football. And great players and great teams can do things to change the momentum of a game in a moment. They can put right what is wrong. They can turn the tide of a match with a tackle, a penetrating run, or a goal from nowhere.

***

Here it comes. Fifteen minutes into the second half. An hour of the match gone. Ryan Giggs down the left. Running like a gazelle. So fleet of foot. Swerves inside Steve Clarke. Clarkey lunges. Giggs stretches and pokes the ball into the penalty box as they both fall to the ground. Dennis Irwin, United's left back, has wandered up field. What is he even doing in the box? It's rolling towards him now. No real danger that far out at that angle, surely? But Eddie Newton dives in. He's committed. 'No, Eddie!!!' He hits the player and not the ball. Up in the air goes Irwin. Up to my head go my hands. I'm right next to Eddie. Eddie – such a good player. Love him as a team-mate. Brave. Skilful. Sacrificial. A big reason I've scored so many goals this season. He always gives me a platform to go forward. A good player. A bad decision. Penalty kick!

Enter Eric Cantona! The first Frenchman to play in an FA Cup final picks up the ball. So calm. So confident. Such style. He wears his collar up – his personal trademark. Every heart in the stadium is racing, but it is as if Eric's pulse slows down. He's living on a different plane. Unaffected. He takes the ball and places it on the penalty spot. Millions are watching around the world. He stands there. Collar up! As if he wants the TV cameras to pan around him and the whole world to take a good look. Dennis Wise is our captain. He's a cheeky fellow. He goes up to Eric. 'Fifty quid says you miss!' Cantona waves him away – like a king with a commoner. He steps to the edge of the box. He stands. Collar up! Dimitri Kharine is in goal. Our Russian keeper has springs in his legs. He's had a great season. Some days he's unbeatable in training. 'Come on Dimi! You've got this!' I shout. But deep inside I have a sinking feeling. Chelsea fans are whistling to a crescendo: like white noise.

***

Penalty takers are a special breed. It takes technique but it is more about nerve for the '12-yard men'. The pressure is huge. It's all on the kicker. I take penalties. I know. It's you against the goalie but – more than that – it is you against yourself. A penalty is scored or missed in the mind of the player before he even kicks the ball. The best players in the world have fallen prey to the pressure. Choose your spot, choose your technique, head down, don't look for the ball to hit the net, the crowd will tell you that. Confidence is king for the '12-yard men'.

***

Referee, David Ellery, places the whistle to his lips. Cantona checks his collar. He runs. Kharine is set. But Eric strokes the ball powerfully with the side of his foot and sends Kharine the wrong way. It's as if he's on the practice ground. The ball hits the back of the net. 1-0. Chelsea whistling is drowned out by the thunder of the United roar. It feels like a waterfall crashing all around us. Ince is on Cantona's shoulders. Adrenalin visibly surges through the Reds. As in normal life, so it is in football. Setbacks often say more about your character than when you're doing well. We have resolve. We're down but not out. But we need our player-manager Glenn Hoddle on the pitch. It's time. His skill and his experience will settle us. No sign of him yet though. We play on. United hit us on two quick counter attacks. Cantona breaks down the middle. I can sense more trouble on the horizon.

A long ball splits our defence and now it's a race between Frank Sinclair and Andrei Kanchelskis. The Russian is as fast as they come. No defender can match him usually. Except Frank, maybe. Frank is Eddie Newton's big mate. The two of them are always together. Always joking. Giving each other stick. Two young guns and products of the Chelsea youth system. Frank can 'catch pigeons', as we say: he's that quick.

He's chasing after Kanchelskis, and they're heading towards the penalty box. Shoulder to shoulder they collide outside the box. Kanchelskis goes down as Kharine collects the loose ball. But wait. The referee has blown for a penalty kick again. It can't be! It wasn't a penalty! The contact was outside the box! It wasn't even a foul. What has David Ellery done? He wasn't close enough to see the incident clearly. His linesman hasn't even flagged. This is a game of key moments and crucial mistakes, and Ellery has made the one that might be most costly for us.

***

Referees have a thankless task. They make decisions at top speed under immense pressure, and they are an easy target for blame from the media, fans and players alike. But this time the referee has got it wrong on one of the biggest stages of all. He's a good ref and he's been having a good game, but he will tell me in a conversation years after this day that he would not have made the same decision given the chance again.

***

Ellery points to the spot amidst outrage from our team. The crowd is screaming. Wembley descends into a cacophony. I can't tell the difference between Chelsea protests and Manchester jubilation. Cantona again. Two penalties in one game. This takes nerve. Which side will he place it now? It's mind games between Kharine and him. He puts the ball on the spot. His collar is still up, and so is his confidence. Dennis Wise is quiet. But Cantona remembers Wise's fifty-pound bet on the first penalty, and this time he goes up to Dennis. He looks down at him and says in his deep French accent, 'Double or nothing!' Dennis is left speechless.

Eric smiles and turns away. Sets himself. Checks that collar once more. Strolls up to the ball and sends Kharine the wrong way again in a replica of the first penalty. Wembley erupts. Keane, Ince, Giggs and Hughes surround Cantona. Our protests are useless. Two penalties in five minutes have undone us. The goal stands. And so does King Eric. He stands... upright, smiling, basking in glory. Collar up!

Hoddle is off the bench unzipping his tracksuit now. He's coming on. At thirty-six, the former Tottenham Hotspur, Monaco and England international is still the best player we have. Playing for Glenn has been a dream this season. He was one of my heroes as a kid. I had his poster on my bedroom wall. He is a maestro. It is as if he has a computer in his mind that, in one moment, can assess all the possible passing options on the field and like the supreme quarterback deliver the perfect ball with the perfect weight and spin. Inside or outside of the right or left foot, it matters not to Glenn Hoddle. He should have had 100 caps for England. He was so good.

Glenn is a truly great player. As a professional you can watch a game and pretty much read what passes or moves a player will make. But the great ones do things even you, as a professional, never see coming. Glenn's vision and balance and ability to do the unusual combine to make him literally beautiful to watch. He sees and does things with a football that others can only dream about. Even Cantona respects him. In our early season 1-0 victory against United in the league, Eric is quoted in the newspapers the following day saying, 'Hoddle was like Mozart in a world full of heavy rockers!' It was true. At his best, watching Hoddle is like listening to great classical music. Pure, elegant and balanced. But is twenty-five minutes enough time for him to save us?

He enters the fray. But it's not long before Manchester United play a long ball up the field. Sinclair slips – that rain won't give up! – and Mark Hughes moves in to score. The Welshman, who will become a Chelsea player within two years, puts another nail in our coffin on this day with United's third goal in nine minutes. Our plan to sit back and hit them on the break has now gone. We are trying to get forward in numbers and they are proving themselves to be what they are – the best counter-attacking team around – and a swarming sea of red comes upon us, wave after wave.

We won't give up though. I have a header saved by Schmeichel. But having beaten him twice with winners this season, it's a different story between the big man and me today. Tony Cascarino comes on from the bench in a late attempt to get something back. Wise, Cascarino and Spencer all go close.

We have good character, but it's not enough today. Another United break forward. Brian McClair scores and our hopes of a comeback are finished. From being in control we've been torn apart. It's 4-0.

The whistle goes. I'm a beaten man. Oh, the pain of defeat! Wembley is a place for winners not losers. Sinclair falls to the ground. Spencer is in tears. Inconsolable. I'm numb. I look up. Can't see my wife or my family. Too many people standing. Cantona comes up to me, 'Peacock, well played', he says. He shakes my hand and then walks off relishing his moment. Tall and confident. Collar up.

We regroup as a team and climb the stairs to the Royal Box to collect our runners-up medals. The Duchess of Kent shakes my hand and gives me a gold medallion. As Steve Bruce leads Manchester United up for the trophy, Dennis Wise leads us back down to the pitch. Dennis is a great captain with an iron will. He covered every blade of the Wembley grass today. We walk round to our fans to applaud them. They are still singing for us. They are rock solid. More tears. They deserve better. I feel the weight of that. However, in time the fans will receive better. This is a start of something new at Chelsea.

***

Three years later I will have left to join QPR, but Chelsea will be back at Wembley to play Middlesbrough in the final. The game will kick off and within a minute Italian midfielder Roberto Di Matteo will break forward and smash a shot against the very same crossbar I hit today. This time it will hit the underside – two inches lower than my effort. This time the ball will go in, and Chelsea will be on their way to years of silverware, which will line the Stamford Bridge trophy cabinets. A Russian billionaire owner. An enigmatic Portuguese manager. And the Blues will rise to become Premier League and Champions League giants.

***

Inches: the fine line between victory and defeat. How might my life have been different if that shot had gone in and we had won? Glenn Hoddle tells us to keep our chins up, but the dressing room is sombre. A bath for tired legs. Media interviews – the last thing I want! Fans waiting for autographs. Forcing a smile through bitter disappointment. Back to the famous Savoy Hotel in London to meet our wives and family and all the Chelsea backroom staff at a banquet. I give my runners-up medal to my dad as a gift – he's my greatest coach. I owe him so much. Mum's there with my sister – loyal as always. The players are resilient. A silly joke to cover the hurt. A bit of laughter. We get through the evening. We'll be back.

***

I finally get to my hotel room at the Savoy. It's just Amanda and me now. We talk as only husband and wife do. I tell her how I feel. Only she truly knows. A footballer is just an ordinary man with ordinary feelings, subject to extraordinary pressures. A lot has happened to us this past year. Promotion to the Premier League, a big move to Chelsea, lots of goals, our first baby. A traumatic birth, cancer, death. We've climbed high mountains and walked through deep valleys together. But there is much to be grateful for. God is sovereign and good. We have each other. We have a son. I lie back on the bed, every muscle aching, the roar of Wembley still rings in my ears. The schoolboy dream. Blues *v* Reds. Over and over I relive the shot that came so close. So, so close. Inches! The Wembley roar fades. Exhaustion overcomes me. Finally, I sleep.

2

EARLY DAYS: LIFE IN A FOOTBALLING FAMILY

I grew up in a footballing family. The smell of the dressing room, the thrill of Saturday match day, and the roaring crowds were part of my upbringing. My father, Keith, played for Charlton Athletic in South East London nearly 600 times – more than any other outfield player in the club's history. He was also the first ever substitute used in English League football. He was a player, a manager and a coach at the top level for over forty years. My father developed many good players, brought the best out of them and, in many cases, launched their careers: top players like Steve Bruce, Tony Cascarino, Mickey Adams and others owe much to my dad. But none was influenced by him more than me.

He met my mum, Lesley, in the late 1950s at Erith Grammar School in Kent, England. Dad was what you call an all-round sportsman and a true leader. He captained the cricket and football teams, was an outstanding athlete and held the school record for the pole vault: a record that stood for many years after he left. My mum was fiercely intelligent and highly fashionable, often seen in her schooldays sporting a cutting-edge beehive hairdo! She was quite the beauty, and still is. My parents weren't born in the same country, but providence played its part to bring them together across an ocean. How they came to meet and marry is a story made for the movies.

My father was born in Barnehurst, Kent, to Thomas and Lydia Peacock on May 2, 1945, just before the end of the Second World War – two days after the death of Adolph Hitler. He was one of two children, my Aunt Valerie being the other. His upbringing was working class. During the hostilities my grandad served his country on a Royal Navy minesweeper. But after the war work was sparse in his hometown of South Shields near Newcastle upon Tyne, so they moved south, and he got a job on the assembly line for Ford automobiles in Dagenham. To think that for the first few years of my dad's life the country remained on wartime rations – a concept that would seem so alien to many of us today!

My grandparents were part of what many refer to as the Greatest Generation: those born between 1901 and 1927 – the parents of the baby boomers. They were people of character: people who knew how to do without because they had to; yet they were always grateful and hardworking folk. As time went on, my grandad worked overtime and grueling night shifts at Ford to pay for luxuries like a car and a TV. My grandparents knew what service and sacrifice meant, especially because of the cost paid by their generation to protect England and mainland Europe from the grip of Hitler's oppression, thus securing many of our freedoms today. So, my father was born into a new and hopeful era and grew up with a good work ethic and a Churchillian sense of love for his country.

My mother's early childhood couldn't have been more different to my father's. She was born in Calcutta, India, on March 8th 1946 during the time of the British Raj. Her father, Leslie Lane – my grandfather – worked for the Calcutta Police. Her mother, Barbara – my grandmother – worked as a hairdresser. They led quite a privileged life, as did many Anglo-

Indian expats – having maids and other house help was the norm.

In the 1940s, summers in the Himalayas, tiger hunts and big band dances were the order of things for expats. When we were small, I remember my grandfather entertaining my sister, Lauren, and me with stories of his encounters with big game during jungle expeditions. His tales of lying in wait in the trees of the jungle and hearing the roar of the tiger in the night conveyed the exciting, exotic and romantic nature of one of the most definitive times in India's history. But good times for the Brits were not to last. By the time my mother had turned three years old, the political situation in Calcutta became extremely unstable. Mahatma Gandhi was on the rise to political prominence in the early 1940s and had already made his famous call for the British to 'Quit India' in 1942. In addition, there was infighting between the Hindus and Muslims, a situation which exploded one day in a very personal way for my grandparents in 1948.

They lived in a fine apartment building in Calcutta City. One afternoon they were on the balcony as fighting between rival religious groups broke out in the street below. The atmosphere was febrile. However, what my grandparents didn't know was that members of those same groups had climbed to the rooftop of their apartment building and the conflict was continuing above. My mother, just a toddler, was playing in the corner of the balcony deck, whilst my grandparents were anxiously watching the events going on below. Suddenly something dropped from the rooftop, flew past their heads and hit the street in front of their eyes. To their horror they saw that it was a small baby! Immediately my terrified and traumatised grandmother turned to my grandfather in horror and said, 'If they are doing that to each other, it won't be long before they come for us.' They both looked at my mother playing away innocently, and in an instant the decision was made.

Within two weeks they were leaving India. Because of my grandfather's contacts in the police, he paid someone a small fee and quickly acquired passports. Now, where to go? They wanted to go to America, but the ship was full and another wouldn't be along for a while. The only other vessel leaving Indian shores was heading for England. There was space. Tickets were purchased. And that's how my mum ended up in Kent, England, living only a few miles from my father in Barnehurst and destined to meet him just over a decade later. One parent from the exotic land of India, one from the historic land of England; both born around times of epic national turmoil in their respective countries. But out of turmoil, love was predestined and from that love I would be born.

My parents knew of each other at senior school, but it wasn't until Christmas Eve in 1961 that they started dating. My mum was hosting a party at her house and my dad gatecrashed. The irony of it all was she had arranged the party in the hope of getting an old boyfriend back. He didn't turn up, but my father did and at one point saw my mother crying on the stairs (because her devious plan had failed!). With all the confidence in the world, he sat down next to her and opened with a killer chat up line, 'Tell me your troubles.' It worked. She poured out her heart. They began dating. And the rest is history, as they say. In fact, over fifty years later my dad says she is still telling him her troubles!

This is how they began their relationship on the way to marriage, although they didn't get down the aisle without some drama. In 1964 my grandparents decided to move to Australia and even though my parents had just become engaged to each other my mum, age eighteen, was made to go. It was a move that was never going to last and after a few months, against her parents' wishes (though they would follow her to England shortly after), my mum boarded a ship and returned to my dad. Once again, they were brought together from across the seas. Even an ocean couldn't stop the commitment and consummation of true love.

They were married on the 10th July 1965. Dad looked sharp in a navy, Beatles-style suit, his hair – short back and sides – was Brylcreem-ed and swept back on top. Mum was stunning in white: her striking, dark eyes still sparkle in the wedding photograph I have on the dresser in our bedroom. My mum's dark hair and eyes reveal her heritage. I always say I got my looks from her and my football ability from my dad!

In many ways, my parents were a product of their culture: a quintessential 1960s couple. Their wedding made the newspapers – 'Football Star Weds Local Girl'. Their photo gives the sense of good days, days of new beginnings: post-war days of icons and iconic achievements: The Beatles, Elvis, Marilyn Monroe, James Dean, JFK, George Best, Pelé, and Muhammad Ali; England winning the World Cup, men landing on the moon, and colour TV. My parents loved each other, and they loved my younger sister, Lauren, and me. If there is one thing I knew, it was that I was loved. Consequently, I grew up with great love and respect for my parents.

My mum was born to be a wife and mother. It was and still is her greatest joy. In some ways she stands in stark contrast to this day and age that often devalues marriage and, in many quarters, sees motherhood as an inconvenience. She nurtured and took care of Lauren and me. And to this day, if ever I'm sick, I will think of my dear mother and her tender kindness and warmth that always seemed to make everything okay. My father was a dad who was affectionate, consistent and present. His job afforded him time with us, and he made sure he gave it to us. He played with us, cared for us and he trained us.

Both my parents disciplined us, but my father took the lead. My sister and I rarely got away with disobedience, but I needed a firmer hand than Lauren. I feared to displease my parents but that healthy fear rested on a foundation of being loved and of knowing they were always fair, patient and very forgiving. They worked on the principle that loving discipline actually gave us freedom. They didn't act like our mates or our peers, they acted as they should – as our parents. Over half a century later, they are still married. Their art of parenting is rare nowadays; in my opinion that is to the detriment of the family in society. Whatever your thoughts on parenting techniques, I feel privileged to have had such a mother and father.

***

My mum gave birth to me on November 18th, 1967. I was 9lbs 7oz. Dad was present at the birth: a new thing in those days, when men didn't even attend prenatal classes. It showed. She was in labour, and he was given the task of administering the gas and air. However, distracted by the sports section of the newspaper he was reading, he kept the mask on her too long. She was almost passing out and, blissfully unaware, he continued reading about the football fixtures for the next day. Consequently, I had a slight blue tinge when I was born…or so they say!

From the moment I could walk I was kicking a ball. The old family cine films show me toddling along and someone from off screen (obviously my father!) throwing a ball in front of me, so that I literally stumbled onto it. I have early memories of my dad taking me to Charlton Athletic's home ground, the Valley, in the school holidays to watch the team train. He would be out on the field with the team and would leave me in the care the physio, Charlie Hall. Those were the days when the physio didn't need much official qualification except that he could run on the field and administer the 'magic sponge' when there was an injury. I liked hanging around with old Charlie because he would often give me a bottle of orange pop from a little cupboard in the back of the physio room. What a treat! Funny the little things you remember as a kid.

Of course, as a young lad, I could only watch training for so long before I myself was kicking a ball around in the tunnel area, climbing the massive Valley terracing or looking around the stadium for Lucky, Charlton's resident black cat. Then I'd be off into the treatment room to see what machines Charlie was hooking up to the players. The players all knew me and would have a chat with me. Some of them, like defender Paul Went and his wife Wendy, used to baby-sit my sister and me. They were like family. As I grew older and began to play for my primary school team, I would have a running competition for goals with striker, Derek Hales. 'How many did you bag this week Gav?!' he'd often say. Derek was a Charlton legend and a prolific goal-scorer. An encouraging word from him and team stars, Mike Flanagan, Colin Powell and others, went a long way to help stoke the fiery ambition in a young lad's heart: even a desire to pull on that red and white shirt one day and follow in my dad's footsteps into the professional game. Little did I know that playing for Charlton Athletic would one day finally come true, if only very briefly.

Dad was Charlton's captain. He joined the club as a seventeen-year-old straight out of school and was in the first team within weeks. The crowd loved him: he was an honest, hardworking, skilful, player who knew where the back of the net was and who would regularly craft out goal-scoring opportunities for his team-mates. He started off as an old-fashioned winger, an 'outside left' they called it. But as he got older he moved inside to a more central, midfield role. He was a general on the field.

He could organize and inspire by example and by his words. Fans and players alike respected him.

Nevertheless, as a professional sportsman, you are a target for much public criticism as well as the recipient of much praise. Public people get public criticism. Your work life is lived out on a stage and everyone feels they have the right to say exactly what they want about you. My father was no exception, and although I was shielded from much of it, I sometimes heard abusive comments from some fans in the stadium as I sat next to my mum and sister on a match day. Mum never reacted to it and remained calm even if my father was being bad mouthed, but I knew it hurt. I remember one incident many years after he had finished his playing career and was manager of Gillingham FC. We were all walking away from a match together – my parents, my sister and me – when a fan accosted my father and abused him to his face about the team's performance and his performance as a coach. My father kept his cool when others would have lost it. He knew that the wrong reaction from him would put his wife and children in danger. This prepared me well for what lay ahead in my own career.

My dad was my greatest coach, and I've played for some good ones. From a young age, he taught me the basics of the game and more than that, the basics of character – the character that would give me the foundation to play the game. We spent hours in the back garden of our little house in Welling. He would have me dribbling the ball in and out of several old red house-bricks, which he would place in a line. He used to place the brick vertically on its smaller end. I not only had to move with the ball in and out of the bricks, I couldn't even touch them. If I did touch one with the ball or my foot, the brick would topple over. The idea was to get through the circuit as quickly as possible and without a single brick going over. 'Better to go slower at first but keep that ball under control, than fly through quickly and knock every brick down.' He was teaching me control and balance. 'Use both feet, not just your right.' And off I'd go. Again, and again. Then we were kicking the ball against the side of the garden wall. Right foot. Left foot. Kick. Control the ball. Kick.

'Okay now let's teach you to head it. Don't be afraid of the ball. Attack it with your head. Top of the forehead. That's it. Eyes open. Mouth closed, so you don't bite your tongue.'

Nowadays, in some quarters, there is a call to ban heading from football, because of long term damage to the brain, etc. I do understand the concern, but heading is one thing that makes football unique. What other sport exists where you use your head to direct the ball? Certainly, due diligence must be done. Research must be carried out. But footballs are lighter than ever now, and it seems there is not enough evidence currently to change this ingredient of the game. In fact, if they do, the face of football will change forever, and in my opinion, not for the better. Don't take heading out of the game; teach kids how to head the ball properly. I wasn't tall. Heading wasn't my strong point. But looking back I actually scored quite a few goals with my head and I could pass the ball with my head adequately; all because technically I could head correctly.

My dad was also a very good juggler of the football. He could keep it up in the air over two thousand times using all parts of his body. Inside and outside of the right foot or left foot, head, shoulders, chest. I spent hours and hours emulating this until I could beat his record, but also so I could be comfortable with the ball at any angle. Finally, I exceeded my dad's record. But more than that, my 'feel' for the football became very good. My dad never let me win anything easily. I had to earn it. So, whenever I did beat him, I knew it was a genuine victory. But he was always secretly glad when I won – as are most dads with their sons. A dad always wants his boy to surpass what he did, something I didn't always fully realize or appreciate, until I had my own son.

His coaching helped me to develop as a technically sound player. I wasn't the biggest kid on the block. But when I played with the older boys I could hold my own because I could handle the football and I could handle my temper. My dad taught me to control the football, but also to control myself. If I ever showed frustration, he would take me aside and teach me that anger wasn't the way to succeed. If I persisted, he would discipline me. He wouldn't hang around outside to coach me if I continued to show my temper. In fact, one of the best lessons both my parents taught my sister and me was never to petulantly feel sorry for ourselves. I soon learned the foolishness and futility of anger and instead learned the value of self-control on the football field. I began to channel any passion and aggression I had into my technique and into my game in a positive way. In this way failures and setbacks became spurs to press on and succeed.

My dad also taught me to be courageous. Can you teach your children courage? I think so. Courage is not the absence of fear but the resolve to face and overcome the thing you fear. He was always encouraging me to try things that stretched me and took me out of my comfort zone. Whether that was making a speech in class, entering swimming galas or sports days, or trying out in talent shows on holiday, he'd say, 'Have a go. Don't be afraid of losing.' The fear of physical pain, defeat, or looking bad in front of others is a big reason why so many kids don't attempt things. I realize, of course, that different children have different propensities; some are predisposed to being more sensitive than others or some are naturally more ambitious than others. And some children need a firmer hand than others to achieve the same results. But parents who coddle their children so that they are never exposed to the possibility of getting hurt don't actually help them.

It is good for a child to lose sometimes, maybe even to face some embarrassment or physical pain. It is the context in which resilience is built. You don't become resilient by always experiencing or expecting to experience good things. But a hedonistic, 'felt-needs' society where children are spoiled by helicopter parents who fly in to fix every moment of discomfort for their child, develops a generation of young adults who tend to lack resilience and consequently an inability to bravely face their fears.

The popular modern-day practice in sports days where winning is banned in over half of UK schools is disastrous. One of the great things about sports is it teaches children that you don't always win, and you cannot always win. Life is not like that. Sheltering children from the possibility of defeat produces a soft underbelly and unrealistic expectations of life. It is good for children to face things they fear. To have physical and moral courage is a noble trait that we should cultivate in our children. Cowardliness is not a good thing in any child and doesn't bode well for them becoming useful members of a society. In contrast, parents who encourage their kids to face the difficult and scary things whilst providing the reassurance of unconditional love help develop bold creativity in the next generation.

I learned a good lesson in courage one year. We were at Pontins holiday camp in Wales. I was around ten years old. On the list of daily camp activities one afternoon there was a kids' boxing competition. The age range was ten to eleven years old. 'Do you fancy this Gavin?' my dad said. 'Yeah okay', I answered. The organizer paired me with a lad my own age but a little smaller than me, and as I looked at him when we lined up he looked really nervous. I was happy with this – I was strong for my age and an easy victory lay ahead. The thing is he ran off and they replaced him with a lad a year older and much bigger than me. Now I was the one quaking in my boots. I didn't run, but I got an absolute pasting. I remember coming out of the ring a little ashamed, a little bruised, and with a tear in my eye. But I saw my dad looking at me with pride in his. 'Great bravery, son. It didn't matter that you lost. It mattered that you stood up and had a go.' Then he sat me down and gave me a sip of his beer. I felt like I became a man that day.

Standing courageously on principles and doing the right things no matter what the cost is a rare thing. But commitment and loyalty are born out of these things. This kind of moral courage and commitment is a mark of manhood – something we admire in men like Winston Churchill and Teddy Roosevelt. Certainly, my father's seventeen-year career at one club was a testimony to a principled man of courageous, faithful service. Obviously, he didn't have the player-freedom and power that they have nowadays or even in my career. But still he persevered year after year until he retired from playing football in the UK in 1978.

I think that this thing about having a foundation of moral principles is key. Both my parents had clear principles. My sister and I knew where we stood and that gave us security. As a child, I was taught basic principles of behaviour and, as a young footballer I was well schooled in the basic principles of the game. The best players and the best teams do the basic things consistently well (and that principle can be transferred to all spheres of life). People were always amazed when they'd come and watch us train at Chelsea Football Club, because we spent the first half hour doing fundamental passing, control and skill drills. They expected us to be far more sophisticated than this. But we knew that consistency in the basics gave us the platform to do the extra things needed to win matches.

Nevertheless, to win you must take risks. In general, people who play life safely live unfulfilled lives. They never move beyond what is comfortable. They are too afraid of failure. Risk was part of my childhood. Although I played football from a young age, I wasn't in organized teams until I was eight. I was out kicking a ball around with my friends in my local park in Welling. But I was also out climbing trees, 'scrumping' (the childhood pursuit of taking apples from a neighbour's tree and then avoiding the owners or the local bobby on the beat) and riding my bike with my friends on long summer days until only hunger pains would force me home. It's a shame that nowadays a combination of 'stranger danger', increased traffic and maybe some over-cautious parenting has led to the curtailment of this kind of freedom especially in the suburbs and cities. I understand the desire for safety, and I am not promoting recklessness, but children need to learn risk. To eliminate this is to stifle creativity and growth, resulting in unproductive underachieving adults.

We need to cultivate that element of risk and adventure, particularly in boys. Nowadays the boy with low attention span and high energy levels is too quickly labelled with ADHD, medicated and subdued, rather than loved, disciplined and encouraged to channel that energy in the right direction. It seems to me that we jump eagerly to the medicine cabinet rather than put in the effort of training and creating avenues for a boy's natural tendencies. Certainly, I do not advocate law breaking (scrumping is not to be encouraged!). However, I think children benefit from learning to assess and take risks. 'Will that branch hold me if I step onto it?' 'Can I make that jump on my bike?' And they try and sometimes fail. And they get hurt and hopefully learn for the next time – or if you are wise you will. As the book of Proverbs says: 'Like a dog that returns to its vomit is a fool who repeats his folly.' Part of growing in wisdom is to be able to assess risk and know when to take it, so as to break new ground.

So, at the feet of my father and in a loving and disciplined home with a caring mother at its heart, and in the playground of the streets and fields, I learned these key lessons of self-control, courage, moral principles and risk-taking which served me well on and off the field of play. I wouldn't have achieved the things I did without that kind of training.

3

ACHIEVING THE GOAL: THE SCHOOLBOY DREAM

When I was young, I used to get up early on a Thursday morning and rush downstairs in my pyjamas where I would find the newspaper poking through the letter box in our front door. Peeking its head out of the centre of the paper was my weekly *Roy of The Rovers* comic. In the UK they say that making it as a professional footballer is the schoolboy dream. Comic books helped cultivate these dreams. From the 1950s, football comics and stories were devoured by young boys all over Britain, but *Roy of the Rovers* was the best and most popular. Roy Race was the star of the comic and the heroic centre forward who played for Melchester Rovers. His team were either challenging for the championship, playing in cup finals or battling for survival. Mid-table risk-free mediocrity was not on the menu for Melchester.

Roy's adventures even took him to foreign lands, where the team faced adversities and adventures – they were sometimes kidnapped by the bad guys. Roy was even shot once, but not killed. Roy's career highlights were when he played for England, but whether he was playing for Melchester or England against foreign opposition, he was always portrayed as possessing good moral character versus the opposition's often cowardly tactics.

Such was the cultural influence of the comic that the phrase, 'It's a Roy of the Rovers performance' made its way into the commentary boxes of the professional game and was used to describe that great moment of skill in a match or the brave comeback and victory against all odds. All this reflecting a post-war age and a post-war British attitude.

England had won the World Cup in 1966 only a year before I was born and captain Bobby Moore was the country's Roy of the Rovers. Kevin Keegan would follow the trend. And, in my era as a player, Alan Shearer and David Beckham would be those men. Cristiano Ronaldo and Lionel Messi epitomize the spirit in the global game today. With England as one of the top football nations in the world, boys played football in the streets, over the parks and in the schools. I was one. I wanted to be Roy Race. I wanted to be Newcastle United's Malcom Macdonald. I wanted to be Liverpool's Kevin Keegan or Manchester United's Brian Robson or Tottenham Hotspur's Glenn Hoddle. But most of all I wanted to be my dad. And with his living example of all that was good about professional football, a strong and relentless desire to achieve that goal continued to grow in my heart.

I enjoyed school, but even at age ten kicking a ball gave me the greatest pleasure. I'll always remember my first goal for Pelham Primary School. My PE teacher, Mr Horne, played me as a striker that day and the ball fortuitously went in the back of the net off my knee in the second half. I didn't care. I was walking on air. It was the first goal that 'counted' as such. Then I took off. Playing for the school. Playing Sunday football for Teviot Rangers, and then joining the elite St Thomas More. I loved playing for Teviot, but St Thomas More were the best team in the South East of England, and they wanted me to join them. I found myself playing alongside exceptional players like Neil Ruddock, a tall and skinny left midfielder in those days.

Who would have known that Neil would have become one of the best and most feared defenders in the country and go on to play for Liverpool and England! In fact, three other players from that team, including myself, made it as professionals, Michael Marks (Millwall FC) and Brian Horne (Millwall FC) were the other two. I wasn't the best player at all for St Thomas More. Truthfully, I didn't really like it there. The manager, Len Reid, used to shout and scream and moan at players from the touchline. He meant well, but I wasn't used to this. It wasn't my father's philosophy with kids. But it was good for me in one sense. I needed to develop a tough skin and up my game because the road ahead would require it.

When I was eleven and in my last year at Pelham Primary School, I represented my district, North Kent. This was the next step along the road and the level at which scouts from professional clubs would take a look at the best young talent. I was playing for school, district and county – a bright young prospect. I passed my eleven plus – the national schools test – which gave me acceptance to Bexley Grammar School, one of the top academic senior schools in the South East of England. Things were going well. I was on course for success in sport and academics. And then, when everything was going swimmingly, in 1978 we moved – to America!

***

The road to success doesn't always follow your planned path and often doesn't run smoothly. Sometimes it comes after unexpected diversions and difficulties. My journey along this road was no exception. America certainly wasn't on my radar. I was a happy lad at home and school, gradually working my way towards my dream of being a professional footballer. But when my dad retired from Charlton at thirty-four years old, he was offered a four-month contract in Columbus, Ohio as player-coach for the Columbus Magic in the ASL (American Soccer League). Former Sheffield United player, Paul Taylor, thought my dad would add experience to his team and a wise head as his assistant coach. Up for the adventure, my parents crossed the ocean with my sister and me in tow.

At first Lauren and I were excited. My sister and I were good friends and were happy in each other's company, so we weren't lonely. We had our sibling arguments, but we loved each other – no one was more loyal to a brother than she, and I was fiercely protective of her. In reality, the Columbus adventure felt like a long holiday for us. No school for a few weeks is what it meant though our parents did give us homework to do in the apartment that the club rented for us. We wrote short stories, read books and learned about the USA to the point that after a few weeks I could tell you every US state and place it on a map.

It was a summer of long sunny days and a new footballing experience in the American Midwest. The Magic played on a new all-weather surface that wasn't grass. They called it AstroTurf! Match days were full of razzmatazz, popcorn and cheerleaders. If it was a tie, there were even penalty shoot-outs in regular league matches to decide who won: the Americans hated the idea of a draw. After an early injury my father played well enough but with his playing days slowly coming to an end it seemed only natural that he would follow the coaching path. Paul Taylor and he became really good friends; so close that Paul and his wife Vivienne were simply known to Lauren and me as 'Uncle Paul' and 'Aunty Vi'. It was a friendship that would reunite a few years later when the coaching roles were reversed, and my father would bring Paul on board as his assistant at Gillingham Football Club in England.

At the end of the summer, mum took my sister and me back to England because, although the Magic had made the play-offs, I was about to start life at Bexley Grammar School in early

September, and my sister was expected back at Pelham. Normal service was about to resume: family, school and football, I thought. Until a phone call from my father came. The Magic didn't win the play-offs and he was about to catch a plane home to England, when Gordon Jago, head coach of the Tampa Bay Rowdies, asked him to stop by Florida on his way back. My dad phoned us from Tampa. 'How'd you fancy a couple of years in Florida?' The American adventure was to continue a little longer. So, we left England again. But as an eleven-year-old, this time it felt more permanent.

Within a few weeks of that phone call, we had rented out our Barnehurst home, secured our visas, packed our bags and were saying goodbye to family at a farewell party at my aunt and uncle's house. The most emotional moment was when my dad embraced his dad at the end of the evening and I saw a tear well up in my grandad's eye: a moment that I was destined to repeat with my own father thirty years later when, for different reasons, I left UK shores for Canada. The pain of leaving loved ones is some of the deepest hurt a person can know.

Florida is one of the most popular holiday destinations for Brits nowadays, so it seems hard to imagine that back then very few were going there on vacation let alone moving there to live. In November 1979, the four of us arrived in Tampa Bay with four huge suitcases and our Boxer dog, Candy. We felt like pioneers in a new land. Beforehand, when I thought of Florida, I thought of Disneyland, palm trees, beaches and sun. It was all of that and more. Joining the Tampa Bay Rowdies was like going to Manchester United (without the cold rain). They were a big team and they played in the NASL (North American Soccer League). America had caught soccer fever and they were sinking big money into it. The top players in the world were coming to kick start the venture: Pelé, Johan Cruyff, Franz Beckenbauer, George Best were gracing the league. England's

53

Rodney Marsh had left the Rowdies the year before we arrived. But the team was full of excellent players. They played in front of crowds of forty thousand in the Tampa Bay Buccaneers stadium: a beautiful bowl-shaped arena with grass like a carpet.

We stayed in a hotel for the initial few weeks in Tampa. It was the first time I had ever experienced room service. Lauren and I ate hot fudge ice cream sundaes every day. We had never tasted anything like them before. It was like eating something from heaven. Everything seemed bigger and better and tastier in America. When we did move out of the hotel, even our house had a swimming pool. But the honeymoon period didn't last long, and I was soon missing home, family, friends and my football. Moving to a new country is really hard. It took me a while to settle. What would happen to my budding football career? Two years in a country where the schoolboy standard was so much lower than England would surely ruin any chance of making it as a professional if we returned to the UK... wouldn't it?

But strange though it may seem, I enjoyed my football there in that tropical climate. I was a good player in England, but I was far and away the best for my age and two grades above in Tampa. This allowed me to try things with a football that I didn't have the freedom to try at home. I began to dribble with the ball more. I practised audacious tricks in matches. I developed as an individual talent as I played for my school and Saturday teams. We used to kick off at midday in 90 degrees of heat. And I simply ran the show on the field. Add to that, the immense talent that was on display week after week at the Rowdies matches and my desire to play professionally simply continued to grow. I even began to develop my own training sessions. I would be out in the blistering heat honing my skills, dribbling and juggling the ball, but I also learned to push myself physically and hurt my body as I ran and ran and ran. You've got to be able to hurt your body if you are going to become a professional athlete. The old saying 'No pain, no gain' is true. I joined the track club at school and began to run against older boys. I got stronger. I developed power and stamina.

After a while I settled in school and made good friends. I was beginning to thrive in Tampa and I enjoyed the Florida lifestyle with bright, sunny, warm days. My father was popular as a coach and the team was doing well. We also became particularly good friends with the former Tottenham Hotspur player, John Gorman, his wife Myra, and their two children, Amanda and Nick. Scotsman John was a galloping left back, enthusiastic and skilful. He was also best friends with Tottenham Hotspur and England star, Glenn Hoddle who was one of my boyhood heroes. One day my dad took me to work with him, and to my surprise I met Hoddle. The Rowdies were training at the magnificent Tampa Stadium. As I walked out onto the pitch before practice, I saw a good-looking guy with long hair sitting in the middle of the field and keeping the ball in the air with his feet. 'Wow, he's good' I thought. I continued to watch. It was as if the ball was glued to his foot. He never lost control and it didn't drop once. I walked closer. 'Gavin, meet Glenn.' It was John Gorman's voice behind me.

The guy with the ball was Glenn Hoddle. He was out on holiday and visiting John during the English league close season. Before he left Tampa, he gave John one of his England shirts and John let me borrow it for a few weeks. I think I wore it every day even though it was six sizes too big! Little did that twelve-year-old boy know that just over a decade later, Glenn Hoddle would pay £1.25 million to Newcastle United for him – and I would become his first signing for Chelsea Football Club.

In the school holidays my dad would often take my good friend, Todd, and me to the training ground. Todd and I used to help the kit men. We would make up the big tubs of Gatorade for the players; then we'd go out onto the training ground and collect balls, pick up cones, clean boots or do anything we could to be useful to the players and staff. At the end of the session we may get fifteen minutes to take shots at goalkeeper, Winston Dubose, or kick the ball with one of the host of international players: Perry Van Der Beck (USA), the elegant Jan Van Der Veen (Holland), goal-scoring superstar, Oscar Fabbiani (Chile) and sharpshooter, Washington Olivera (Uruguay). I learned how they moved with the ball. I copied their turns and skills. I watched continental flare in the Rowdies' camp, and I began to develop that style in my own game.

I was so privileged to get up close and personal with these stars. It got even better on match days for Todd and me. We were given the job of 'Runners'. The 'Runner' task was to assist the kit man before, during and after the game. We laid out kit, made the drinks, broke the Hershey chocolate bars into bite size pieces (yes, they put chocolate in the dressing rooms in those days), got towels for the players. I loved it, and I had the best role – I was 'Runner' for the opposing team. I knew all the Rowdies' players anyway, so this was a chance to be in the same room as the stars from other teams that visited Tampa. And what a list: Brazilian World Cup winner, Carlos Alberto, Dutch maestros, Johan Cruyff and Johan Neeskins, and the incomparable Irishman, George Best, all graced the Tampa stadium. I would do my work and then listen to the team talks before the game, at half time and after the matches. I brought Best his towels. I gave Alberto his boots. I sat next to Neeskins on the bench. I saw Cruyff smoke a cigarette at half time! At the end of the night, the kit man would give me a few dollars tip, and just before the away team would leave, I would ask for autographs from these players. For a twelve-year-old, it was a fantasy world. That was my life for two years: family, school and football – I even learned to appreciate the Rowdies' quirky marketing motto: 'Soccer is a kick in the grass!'

A year into our Florida adventure, I travelled to Texas to meet up with my old Sunday team, St Thomas More, who were playing in the Dallas Cup. It was good to see Neil Ruddock and co. again. But after twelve months away it was also good to see how I had grown (or not) as a player compared to them. I did okay. I actually hadn't lost ground. I was now loving the Florida good life along with the rest of my family. In my first year, I played for the Temple Terrace Terrors – yes that really was their name! But in my second year I played for the Tampa Bay Rangers coached by ex-Scottish professional, Alex Pringle. Pringle and his assistant Bobby Dodds, another Scotsman, were true characters and good coaches. They understood the game and they gathered the best boys in the area together. We combined discipline with talent and achieved well, playing expansive football in the league and cups in which we competed. It was a thoroughly enjoyable experience – and just the way kids' football should be organized and played.

Todd and I played in midfield together for the Rangers. We were the best of friends. In the school holidays we would constantly be at each other's houses setting up football matches in the living room. We draped bed sheets over the back of two sets of two chairs placed at either end of the room. And with a jug of iced water in the fridge for refreshment and pretending to be our favourite players we played for hours with a sponge ball. We'd chat on the phone about the match on Saturday, the latest Adidas boots on the market and maybe the latest pretty girl at school. But football ruled in our lives – even over girls. We lived for football. These were special days for me. And Todd became the brother I never had.

The Rowdies was a big family and the players and wives were friends. My parents also made relationships through our schoolmates. Lauren became good friends with a girl called Stacie Berger. Her sister Allison was closer to my age and at school with me. Their father, Lewis, was a plastic surgeon in town. He and his wife Ileana became friends with our parents and the Berger family became very dear to us. To this day I still visit Lewis and Ileana whenever I am in Florida with Amanda. And our children view them as 'second grandparents'. It's rare in life to find good friends, yet those two years in Florida yielded a few of the very best for us.

I hoped we'd spend longer in Tampa. But towards the end of his two-year contract with the Rowdies my father was offered the Gillingham FC manager's job. This third division club in the county of Kent was an ideal opportunity for him to cut his teeth as the 'number one' at an English club. It all happened pretty quickly again. It's that way in football. One minute you're there. The next you're gone. Hardly time to say goodbye. It was like that: a few phone calls, the last game of the season, my dad on a flight back to England leaving my mum, sister and me to sell the house and pack up everything.

I often think back and remember my mother's bravery and fortitude as a young woman. At nineteen, leaving Australia on her own to return to my father in England. Leaving England with her husband and young children to forge a new life and make a home for us in a foreign land. Left to tie up loose ends on her own when my father needed to go back to England at the drop of a hat. Sometimes when we see our parents as they get older and are past the peak of their powers, we tend to forget they did things and dared things and overcame many obstacles, as they blazed a trail for us long before we ever achieved anything. And so often it is a trail we, as their children, have benefitted from richly. My mother has many great qualities that served us well and which I admire greatly. My father got the headlines, but my mother was his great helper and a practically wise homemaker. My dad often borrows a line from the Bette Midler song to describe my mum and says to her, 'You are the wind beneath my wings!' And so she was, and so she still is to this day.

Our time in Tampa came to a close and with many tears we left that bright and sunny land and returned home to Kent, England, and to a new chapter. And after a detour in the sun, now at age fourteen, things were about to take off for me!

***

When you leave your homeland and move to another country, and if you return, you can often experience what they call 'reverse culture shock'. You've gone through all the homesickness, disorientation and difficulties in adjusting to a new culture. Then you return and, although your homeland might be the same, you are not. When you were away, you missed many things about 'Home', but you also grew to love many things about your new country as you adapted and settled. You have friends there. Some history also. And so, the same feelings you experienced when you left home the first time, you experience when you come back home – reverse culture shock.

I had a dose of that when we landed back in London in the summer of 1981. Everything seemed so dark and small in England after two years in Florida. Dark skies instead of sunny skies. Dark, small rooms in our 100-year-old red brick Barnehurst house instead of the bright open plan of our brand new Tampa abode. Narrow windy roads and tiny car park spaces instead of wide straight roads and plenty of room to park your truck. School took a bit of getting used to as well. School in Tampa (Berkeley Prep) was a very good standard of education but much more relaxed. Now I was in a top English

Grammar School with rigorous academics and strict discipline. School uniform. Daily assembly. Hymn singing. Standing when a teacher entered the classroom. Boys called by their surnames. Girls called by their Christian names. The cane. Walking on the left side of the corridor only. If you forgot, you might feel a teacher's hand on the scruff of your blazer hauling you across to the other side.

But my school – Bexley Grammar – not only produced good students it produced useful people. And after a while I loved my time there. The teachers were of the highest calibre. They were not our mates, they were our teachers; they commanded respect, and they knew they had the backing of the parents. If 'Jimmy' was given detention, 'Jimmy' would be given worse by his parents when he got home. My Maths teacher, John Collins, could skilfully hit you with a piece of chalk from fifteen metres if you were talking in the back row of his class. You didn't mess with him. But what a teacher! And how the students loved him. He was a Charlton Athletic fan too. That always helps!

That the teachers maintained their authority didn't mean they were unapproachable or unfriendly though. My Latin teacher, Tony Glover, was a huge football fan. He was from Merseyside and had taught the Liverpool and England player Sammy Lee, who would become my team-mate at QPR a few years later. More than once I was almost late for my next class when, after declining Latin verbs, I was delayed because I was chatting to Mr Glover about the school football results at the weekend or Liverpool's latest victory at Anfield.

David Jones was a strong headmaster, who set the tone for the school. Mr Jones saw it as good and right to publicly celebrate and recognize academic and sporting achievement in school assemblies. And everyone was encouraged to participate in some activity that represented the school. The idea of responsibility and representation was instilled in us at Bexley

Grammar. We were required to wear our school blazers and ties inside and outside of school until we got home. If you were seen on public transport minus your blazer or tie you might be disciplined. That seems too much when we talk about it today, but we were taught to remember at all times that we represented our families and the school. The idea was to develop a sense of other-centredness and service. The overall aim was to develop a responsible, outward-looking student.

Unless you give kids responsibility at times, they will not learn to take moral responsibility of their own accord. Being captain of the school football team taught me a lesson in moral responsibility. We reached the semifinals of the regional schools' cup. We had a big lad who played striker, Jason Honeyman. Jason was a very talented all-round athlete but could be, shall we say, a little temperamental and rebellious at times and would cause the sports master, Peter Jacques, a few problems. To play for the school you had to make school practice sessions in the week. Simple. In the week before the semifinal, Jason hadn't been turning up. Here was a dilemma. Do we ignore the principle and play him because he is one of our best players or do we play Paul Marchant, who wasn't as good as Jason, but had solid character and was a loyal and committed member of the school team? Mr Jacques handed me the responsibility, 'What do we do? You are captain and I'm letting you decide.'

Paul was my good friend, we'd been mates since we were seven years old and played for Teviot Rangers together, and I knew it might look like a case of favouritism if he played. But I also knew what was right, so I voted to leave Jason out and play Paul. Mr Jacques backed me. We lost the match that week. Certainly, Paul didn't let us down. But maybe we would have won with Jason playing. Nevertheless, the principle of the thing was upheld. I was disliked by Jason and his friends for quite a while after that. Hopefully they've forgiven me by now!

In those days I learned a lesson about the cost of taking moral responsibility and making decisions. It is not easy. Nevertheless, my assessment of Paul's character wasn't wrong. After leaving school he proved himself in the world of business and is now CEO of Primark, a multi-billion-pound company and one of the UK's leading clothes retailers with a 17 per cent market share. His reputation is one of integrity and talent, and he is genuinely one of the industry's good guys.

I'm glad for the teachers I had and the influence they had over me and others at Bexley Grammar School. The school motto *'Praestantiae Studere'* means Strive for Excellence. And excellence of academics and character was the aim. That was the way it was then. But much has been lost with the usurping of teacher authority, the advent of student rights and the increase of parental abdication. This, in a world of pop psychology that has undermined right authority structures and created a culture of entitlement instead of gratitude and obedience. It's almost absurd to think that Mr Collins and co.'s style would perhaps lose them their jobs nowadays. Of course, styles do change, and teaching methods change. They were different in the 1980s than they were in the 1920s. But teaching principles should not change. My school wasn't perfect by any means. But I think I benefitted from a good era in the English school system.

The 1980s were in full flow when I returned to Bexley Grammar from Tampa. Michael Jackson was revolutionizing pop videos with Thriller, the title track of his best-selling album. Madonna was shocking us with her boldness. Duran Duran, The Police, Spandau Ballet, Wham, Bananarama, Queen and Lionel Richie were whom we listened to daily. And Bruce Springsteen was 'The Boss'. Rah-rah skirts for girls and Farah trousers with Lyle and Scott sweaters and tie-pins for boys were what we wore. And as for the hair! Big was beautiful! Not only did the girls backcomb and perm, the guys wore their hair long too. The 1980s was the era of some of the worst mullets in history. And I'm not just talking about Tottenham Hotspur and England player Chris Waddle. Yet even with his most forgettable haircut, Waddle was joined by his Tottenham Hotspur team-mate, Glenn Hoddle, on BBC One's iconic *Top of the Pops* as they sang the mildly nauseating song, 'Diamond Lights', in front of millions! Actually, Glenn had a really good voice! However, if music and fashion set the general tone for a generation, football was still king and players were not only the superstars, they were on the verge of becoming the super-rich.

***

The 1990s were a few years away. But with the '90s would come the introduction of Sky TV, and the Premier League. The combination of TV sponsorship and the Premier League package would generate big money in the game. Enter a man called Jean Marc Bosman. Bosman, who played for RFC Liege and earned several Belgium Youth international caps, would not be remembered for what he won on the field of play but for what he would win off it.

At the end of his contract in 1990, Liege would hinder a move for him to join Dunkerque in France by asking a prohibitive transfer fee which Dunkerque would not meet. Bosman would be out of the first team, would receive a wage cut and remain trapped at Liege. But he would bravely take his case to the European Court of Justice in Luxembourg and sue for 'Restraint of trade'. In 1995 the Court ruled in favour of Bosman and this would mean that players whose contracts expire would be allowed a free transfer and freedom of movement within Europe. This would open the door for multinational domestic leagues with the Premier League being the cream. It will also blow the lid off the wage structures within clubs and they would begin to climb in a seemingly never-ending spiral upwards. Sadly, it would not pan out personally well for Jean Marc: a battle with alcoholism would inevitably end in financial trouble. He would never benefit from the thing for which he fought. But the Bosman Ruling was to have a dramatic effect on the professional game of football, and Jean Marc's surname will go down in football history.

That was to come, but in 1983 this boy from Kent couldn't even imagine those changes or freedoms. My dad had given me a taste of some things that promote, protect and improve the game through his involvement with the Professional Footballer's Association (PFA). The PFA exists 'to protect, improve and negotiate the conditions, rights and status of all professional players by collective bargaining agreements'. My father was not only the PFA representative for Charlton Athletic, he was on the committee in the 1970s alongside World Cup winner, Alan Ball, future Chief Executive, Gordon Taylor, and Chairman, Derek Dougan.

Television, the Premiership, the Bosman ruling and the PFA would all feature to some extent in my career but for now, it was all about passing my GCSEs (General Certificate of Secondary Education) at Bexley Grammar School, playing for England Schoolboys…and edging one step closer to the schoolboy dream.

***

'That could be you next year', my dad said to me as we watched England *v* Scotland Schoolboys on ITV one May afternoon in 1982.

'Really?', I replied.

'Yes, I believe you could do most things if you set your mind to it.'

It's a wonderful thing to be encouraged. Especially by your father. I never forgot those words. In my first year back from the USA, I got onto my school team, my district team and then played at Kent county level. My sojourn in Tampa had only served to increase my appetite and my skill level for the game. And when I hit English shores again, I was flying. Not only was I quicker and stronger, I had individual skill that wasn't there before. All this earned me representative honours and a little interest from West Ham Football Club.

It's different nowadays with the scouting systems at football clubs when they are looking at players from eight years old and all around the world, but back in the '80s the game was less global and more local. Talent scouts from professional teams wouldn't start looking at you until you had reached district or county level quality. County standard was very good, and it was a high honour indeed to be a Kent Schoolboy. My schoolmate, Lewis Robinson, and I both made it through a series of football trial matches and achieved those representative levels.

Millwall snapped up Lewis, a strong, honest defender with a sledgehammer left foot. But West Ham scout, Mike Dove, gave my dad his business card after my first appearance for the county team. I scored. It's funny how you remember certain goals as if it were yesterday. This was an easy one in some ways. The ball was played down the wing and I made a run into the box – the kind that would become a trademark of my professional game. The ball was played across and as it came to me amidst a host of opposition players, instead of hitting it first time, I had the awareness to take a touch, control it and simply pass it into the corner of the net. I'd seen Oscar Fabianni and Washington Olivera do this for the Tampa Bay Rowdies many times. I felt free to try it for the teams I played for out there. In that moment, at the highest level I'd yet played, it just came as second nature. It obviously caught the eye. However, I never joined West Ham as a schoolboy. My father wisely kept me away from signing for any team at that stage. But I still have Mike Dove's card somewhere in a box of treasured keepsakes.

Playing for Kent Schoolboys propelled me into the arena where I competed against Essex and Paul Ince. 'Incey' was loud, chirpy and a great player. He had all the banter. I liked him. He and I came from very different backgrounds. His family life was distorted and dysfunctional. His dad left home when he was very young and his mum went to find work in Germany, leaving Paul and his siblings in London with relatives. He was a winner on the field and, despite his hard upbringing, he found a way out; not by feeling sorry for himself and having a victim mentality, but by working hard and being resilient. Character transcends circumstances. And that is one of the things I love about football. Professional players come from all kinds of backgrounds: rich and poor; middle class and working class. But the field of play levels the players, and character and skill are what count.

Paul and I would go on to England Schoolboy International trials that year. We were selected as two of the best midfielders at county level and began the long road to being chosen to represent our country at age fifteen. The trials consisted of intense weekends of matches and training sessions where FA coaches watched and assessed us. To begin with they were regionally based. Mine was in Nottingham. Just to make it to the Nottingham trials was good. I was nervous. But it was a testing that was necessary. I did well and seemed to be able to hold my nerve under pressure. Then we had to wait to receive a letter telling us if we'd made the next stage. I'd watch for the post each day. Hoping. Until one day a letter came through the door, with the English Schools FA stamp on the front. I opened it nervously. Relief. Joy. I made it through. The final stages were held at Lilleshall Hall National Sports Centre in the middle of the beautiful Shropshire countryside.

I remember getting on the train at London Kings Cross Station and being waved off by my family; meeting some of the other boys from different parts of the South who had made it this far; sleeping in strange surroundings; the question going round and round my head, 'Will I be good enough?' My experience of Lilleshall was made better by the young lad with whom I shared a room. His name – Michael Thomas. Michael was a real help and very kind to me. He had played for England Schoolboys a year earlier. He was that good. Already signed by Arsenal and a certainty to make the final England squad, he advised me on what to expect from each session. At the end of the weekend on our last night, exhausted from giving our all, we turned off the light in our room. And Michael casually said, 'You'll be England's "Number 6" this year Gavin.' He was right. After two more trial weekends, I saw off the competition and received that final letter. Paul Ince didn't make it that year. But he'd be back. He had the character and the skill. However, I was in! An English Schools international footballer.

It's hard to describe the feeling of representing your country at any age. But at fifteen you are still a kid in school. It's remarkable. I was in the throes of studying for the all-important GCSEs. *The Times* newspaper wanted to interview me. I remember being allowed time out of class as they took photos of me juggling a ball on the field, schoolmates watching, almost hanging out of their classroom windows to see the event. The next day I rushed down to the corner shop before school, and I saw my name in the newspaper for the first time.

I was a regular starter for England throughout a season which climaxed in that annual televised game against Scotland at Wembley Stadium. Having dispatched Germany there earlier in the year, we were favourites to win. The game was played out in front of sixty thousand screaming fans. My dad's words from a year before came back to me, 'That could be you.' Now it *was* me. We drew 3-3. That was on Saturday. On Monday I went to school and sat my Maths GCSE, which I was taking a year early. What a contrast that was. The adrenaline rush of international stardom and within forty-eight hours it was regular school exams. It was 1983. My father had purposefully kept me from signing schoolboy forms for any professional team to date. I had been playing enough football and my body needed time to rest and develop as well. But now an England international and the only one in the squad who wasn't signed up, several teams were knocking on my door.

***

Queens Park Rangers probably wasn't the obvious choice. Tottenham Hotspur, Arsenal, West Ham, Aston Villa and Liverpool were bigger clubs and all of them wanted me to sign for them. But QPR had two things I liked. Firstly, they brought a high percentage of young players through their ranks to first team level. And secondly, they had Terry Venables as manager. Venables was hot property. Bright, young, inventive. His teams played football as it ought to be played. He was tactically aware and drew the best out of his players. QPR also had a new state-of-the-art stadium at Loftus Road, and they played on the first ever AstroTurf pitch used in UK top-flight football. I decided to sign schoolboy forms for them with an agreement to turn professional the following year.

My last year at school flew by, full of studies and football. And with ten GCSEs completed I left Bexley Grammar School in the summer of 1984 and joined QPR. At sixteen years old I was now in a man's world in one of the most competitive professions in the world. I'd achieved the schoolboy dream. But the reality was, the work had only just begun.

4

LIKE FATHER LIKE SON

The match-day programme read: 'Gavin is the son of former Charlton stalwart and Gillingham manager Keith Peacock.' That was the line that began my player bio for the first few years of my professional football career. I was known as 'the son of Keith'. Following in the footsteps of a famous father can be very difficult. Of course, following in your dad's footsteps no matter who he is or what he does can be tough. But in days gone by this idea of 'like father like son' was considered a good and noble ambition. 'He's a chip off the old block' was the term used to describe the son who had his dad's characteristics.

The concept of passing on a father's name was tied to his sons, who would hopefully marry and have their own children – the male being key to the continuity of the name. Sons wanted to emulate their dads. Dads wanted their sons to emulate them. Sons often continued in their father's field of work. This meant that very often the family business would be called for example, 'Smith and Son', and the son of Smith would continue the business when his father died. Unfortunately, not every son has a dad whom they desire to emulate. Their dads are not good role models; they've not been present in the lives of their boys and have selfishly pursued their own agenda. Work, hobbies, sport, even the pub have become their gods. The real work of cultivating character and loving and directing their sons has been ignored or considered too difficult. Or sometimes fathers have coddled their sons so much that they never gave them good discipline and consequently created entitled young men. In other tragic cases some boys have only known abusive fathers.

Here we touch on one of the most devastating issues of the past fifty years – fatherlessness. In many places we have an absence of fathers and therefore a father hunger. Obviously, girls are hugely affected, but boys suffer first and foremost because they are lacking male role models. Fathers always set the tone in the home. The question is, just what kind of tone are fathers setting? The traditional purpose of dad being head of the home was not so he could boss everyone around but that he would love his wife and lead his family for their good. True fatherhood involves sacrifice on the part of the man – going the extra mile, doing the hard things, casting moral vision and so on. But sadly, with a radical reimaging of the family, a cultural press to remove men from their roles, a lack of responsibility assumed by young men and the increase of no-fault divorce and broken homes, absent fathers are much more the norm. By absent I don't simply mean physically absent, I mean influentially absent. Boys are growing up without good fatherly influence in their lives. The father who used to be central in the home, using his authority for the benefit of his wife and children, and training his sons to be like him is extremely rare today. And even as I write this, I am aware that it will sound strange to many readers.

My dad was a good father, present in the lives of both my sister and me – as was my mother. Consequently, I had a natural desire to want to be like him and follow in his footsteps, but he did make efforts to cultivate it. Fathers shouldn't be afraid to impress themselves upon their sons, not to be burdensome but in a good way: to pass on what they know, to teach them to be passionate about the things they are passionate about – all the while giving them room for personal expression and preference. Fathers should be training their boys to be men: to have self-control, to work hard at school, to get a job, to treat women with honour and to pursue a wife. Nowadays, marriage is the last thing on many young men's minds. And old virtues like nobility and chivalry are not in the modern masculine vocabulary. In our generation we have many directionless, undisciplined young men who are stuck in adolescence: playing video games, watching pornography and abdicating responsibility. Fatherlessness plays a big part in this.

Football is a microcosm of the culture. Premier League manager, Tony Pulis, pointed out in an interview with BBC Radio in 2015, that sixteen- and seventeen-year-old players were joining his club, and he not only needed to coach them, he needed to mentor them. He noted that they were undisciplined because so many never had fathers in their lives. Former Arsenal and England star, Ian Wright, never knew his father. It was his school sports teacher who was the first form of loving male authority in his life. I've already mentioned Paul Ince. But he has also spoken publicly about the importance of fathers in the lives of their sons.

Within the game of professional football, just as in the culture, we see a critical loss of a sense of responsibility to mentor the young. Reversely there has been a loss of the sense of respect that the young should have for their elders. I watched this trend develop over almost twenty years as a professional footballer. But as I began life as a young QPR apprentice in 1984, things were different. I would go into the first team dressing room with my fellow apprentices, heads down, picking up all the dirty training kit, collecting the boots from the three or four pros each of us was responsible for and then getting out of there quickly. If any of us were fortunate, we'd be given five quid to go and buy some drinks for everyone at the local shop in South Africa Road where the QPR stadium sat. We may even be allowed to keep the change!

The older pros ruled the dressing room at QPR. Our captain, Terry Fenwick, bossed things. You didn't mess with 'Fen'. He was hard but fair – a good player and a strong leader, who commanded respect amongst the players. The youngsters had little say in what went on because the senior players ran the show. Apprentices were there to learn and earn their stripes. If you were too cocky, you'd be cut down quickly. Nevertheless, some of the older pros would still take time with us. England international, John Gregory, took me aside after training one day: 'I've noticed, you're pulling the ball to the left when you shoot.' And then he proceeded to show me what to do. And John could ping a ball straight as a die – as good as anyone around in that day!

Then there was Clive Allen. What a goal scorer he was! I didn't have much time with Clive at QPR before his big move to Tottenham Hotspur. But I watched him carefully. He was a clinical finisher. After training he showed me a routine he practised where he set up six balls on an arc from the corner of the six-yard box to the centre of the D on the edge of the penalty box. He then set a cone one yard inside each of the goal posts on the goal line. Starting on the six-yard box he would take one step and strike the ball in between cone and post, push off backwards and then re-approach the next ball, strike, one step backwards, re-approach and so on until all the balls had been dispatched into the goal accurately and at speed. It was like watching a great snooker player practise his angles on the playing table, developing his skill at placing the balls into the pocket from any direction. I used what I called the 'Allen's

Angles' drill regularly over my career. It developed precision and accuracy.

Gary Chivers, Clive Walker, Mike Fillery – a trio of ex-Chelsea players – looked after me and taught me some of the tricks of the trade. They were all highly talented individuals, but they watched over me. They could see I was keen and maybe a little green behind the ears. In my first days of training during preseason we had a 5 km run. I could run well and flew out ahead of the pack. All the older pros were moaning at me. 'Slow down, Peacock; you nutcase. You'll make us look bad!' Walker and Chivers pulled me aside after the first session. 'Look, you need to pace yourself. Preseason training is a marathon not a sprint.'

They were correct. Midfielder, Gary Mickelwhite, was giving me a ride into training in those early days. We lived quite close to each other in Kent. On the way home that day of the 5K run, with Gary driving his white Ford XR3i, striker, Steve Burke, in the passenger seat and me in the back of the car, my hamstring suddenly went into spasm and completely cramped up. If you've ever had a cramp in the hamstring you know how painful it is. My leg shot out in front of me and I flung myself backwards, smashing my head against the car door and lying rigid and prostrate. 'Craaaaamp!!' was all I could scream. As we drove over Westminster Bridge and past the Houses of Parliament, paralyzed and in excruciating pain, I looked up. All I could see out of the window was Big Ben. And all I could hear was 'Serves you right; you little whippersnapper. Running off like a greyhound in training! You'll learn!' The lads were ruthless. I laugh now. But I wasn't laughing then.

***

My father had trained and prepared me, and I was following in his footsteps and into the professional game. But still I needed to make my own mark – to be my own man. He couldn't do it for me. This was *my* life and *my* time. The car rides with Gary and Steve were a learning curve for me. I'd hear them talk about the game, managers, tactics. I listened and learned about the professional game. I also learned to take criticism and be able to laugh at myself. Footballers live off humour. It's a pressure release as well as being part of the culture. The humour was sharp and cutting and it seemed I was on the receiving end in the early days. But it taught me not to take myself too seriously.

The dressing room is tough, not for the fainthearted. In fact, I saw many a good player not make it because he couldn't handle the banter and criticism in the dressing room. But that was the testing ground. If you couldn't handle it off the pitch, you'd never handle it on the pitch in front of thirty or forty thousand people and with the country's media critiquing you. Not all that is called humour is good, but I think one good effect of sarcasm is that it can work to undercut pride and develop toughness. The banter would fly around the QPR training round. Some of it was hilarious. Nevertheless, some of it wasn't so good. I had the nickname, 'Patel', because of my dark hair and skin. The players thought nothing of it. Just that it was funny. They meant no harm and of course they were unaware of my heritage. But I hated it. Plus, verbal and physical abuse of Pakistanis was rife in the UK in the '80s. Sometimes it is a knife edge between banter and racism. I am no expert on the subject but suffice to say any kind of attitude that elevates oneself in value above another human being based on the colour of their skin or ethnicity is evil. It is dehumanizing.

I can only imagine what kind of blatant racism players like Liverpool great, John Barnes, and many others faced, not only in the dressing room, but from the crowds. The resolve, courage and pure skill of many black players in my generation, but also before and after my time, cannot be overstated. It's hard to fathom the experience of Paul Canoville, who played for Chelsea from 1981–1986, when he says, 'I was abused by my own fans simply for the colour of my skin. Bananas were thrown at me, razor blades sent in the post. Nothing would stop me living the dream as a professional footballer. But the cost almost killed me.'

There was Canoville and Barnes. But even before them there were West Bromwich Albion's Laurie Cunningham, Brendan Batson and Cyril Regis, who were all black men of immense character and ability. Having become the first British player to play for Real Madrid in 1979, and whilst enjoying a good season with Rayon Vallecano ten years later, Laurie tragically died in a car accident in Madrid. He was thirty-three. I would get to know Brendan and Cyril as my life and career unfolded. But all three had a massive impact in forging a path through for black players by smashing stereotypes, because they were simply brilliant footballers with phenomenal courage.

They paved the way for many black players in my generation to break through: Paul Ince, Paul Parker, Des Walker, David James, Andy Cole and many others did their own work but owe much to the men who went before them. I still remember the day Les Ferdinand walked into the QPR training ground. Dave Butler the physio said, 'We've signed a lad from Hayes. He's built like Mike Tyson!' Les was young and had rough edges to his game when he arrived but had the seeds of ability and natural power which would take him to the very top level for club and country. A humble man and a true gentleman, Les would go down as a QPR all-time great and remains my friend today.

***

The early days at QPR presented many challenges. Full-time training when you're sixteen takes its toll. Your muscles take time to develop the steel that endures the rigours of the profession – the intensity and high level of daily training and matches, and the lack of recovery time before you need to go again is relentless. Your body is still developing and yet you are competing against mature men. It's not schoolboy stuff anymore. It's business. The mindset is completely different. People's livelihoods are at stake. The future of families is at stake.

I began to adapt. Over the next year I moved from the youth team to the reserves. I made the England U/17 squad. It was going well. Then I contracted glandular fever! This was not just a challenge – it was a real setback. I couldn't run more than a lap after the initial fever and tonsillitis, I was so exhausted. I wouldn't train for nearly three months. That's a long time when you're seventeen and fighting to make it in the world of professional football. At first, all I could think of was how much ground I was losing. But as the weeks went on and I got a little stronger, I came up with a plan. If I couldn't train with the lads and my aerobic fitness was hindered, then I'd work on my muscular strength. At 5' 9" I needed to be all I could be physically. I inspired myself with Rocky movies and the stories of his comebacks against the odds, which were hitting the screens in the 1980s. I painted the inside of our garage at home and set it up like a small gym, with a bench press and some free weights. I studied diet. I read fitness magazines and I developed a weights programme, which systematically built my muscle mass and power. Over the next few weeks, surrounded by posters of Sylvester Stallone and with Journey playing on my 'ghetto blaster', I went through the pain barrier each day, put on eight pounds of muscle and carved out a new physique. When I eventually came back onto the QPR training ground, though I was a bit ring rusty to start with, I was 20 per cent stronger. I found I could hold players off much more easily.

I was even half a yard faster because of increased leg strength and explosive power.

Again, an unusual turn of events, which could have worked against me, actually worked for me. Life doesn't always flow in the way you think it will, but when it doesn't, the question is how you respond. If you look at David Beckham, Alan Shearer, Steve Gerrard, Ryan Giggs and many others, you see that they all battled through adversity. It is the same with all successful people.

***

It was at this time that I became a Christian. I'd been increasingly thinking about life and its great purpose. I mean, I had everything, didn't I? I had achieved the schoolboy dream. I had money in my pocket at a young age. I potentially had a good future. I had relative fame compared to many of my contemporaries who had left Bexley Grammar School. These are all the things that are meant to give ultimate satisfaction – all the things the magazines and newspapers promote to young people: the fame, the popularity, the money, the career. But for some reason I wasn't really that satisfied. Because football was my god: if I played well I was up, and if I played badly I was down. My sense of well-being depended entirely on my performance. I loved football. But I soon realized that achieving this goal wasn't all it was cracked up to be. I was still struggling to find purpose, so I decided to attend a local Methodist church one Sunday evening. Truthfully, I only went because my mum decided to go along, and I thought I'd keep her company. I don't remember exactly what the Reverend Alistair Bolt said in his sermon that night, but after the service he invited me to his house, where he and his wife, Jane, hosted a weekly youth Bible study.

That evening I walked into a room full of young people as the one with money, career and fame. I even rolled up in the car I had bought, a 1980s icon, the Ford Escort XR3i. I was part of the 'in crowd', and they were not. Yet when they spoke about Jesus, they displayed a life and joy that I did not have. They talked about sin as if it had consequence and about God as if they knew Him. I was a Moralistic Therapeutic Deist before the term was coined. In other words, I thought God, if He existed, was simply there to help me with my difficulties and make me happy, and that if I were a good person I'd go to heaven.

I decided to return to the Bible study the following week and the next, and I began to hear the gospel for the first time. I realized that my biggest problem wasn't whether I met the disapproval of a 20,000-strong crowd on Saturday; my biggest problem was my sin and the disapproval (in biblical terms, 'wrath' or 'judgement') of almighty God, who had made me and owned me. I realized that the biggest obstacle to happiness was that football was king instead of Jesus, who through His death on the cross provided forgiveness of sins, release from the judgement of God, eternal life and the promise of heaven. God, in His great love and grace, had done for me what I could never do for myself through the life, death and resurrection of Jesus, His son.

I realized what the great theologian, Augustine, had expressed many years before in his book *Confessions*: 'Thou hast made us for thyself, O Lord, and our heart is restless until it finds its rest in thee.' Over the next few weeks my eyes were opened through those Sunday meetings, and I turned and believed the gospel. And everything changed. Life wasn't ultimately about me anymore; it was about God and His purposes. His purposes involved me, but they didn't end with me.

I was open with my QPR team-mates and immediately told them I had become a Christian. Their reaction was a mixture of mockery and intrigue. Then they watched to see if my life matched my profession of faith. I had found my centre and my purpose. I could now enjoy football for what it was. My heart still burned for football, but now it burned for Jesus Christ more. And He ultimately shaped my life from then on. We'll return to this later.

***

Back in the reserves at QPR my fellow youth player, Gavin Maguire, and I were really progressing well. Gavin and I had both joined QPR as fifteen-year-old schoolboys and risen through the ranks together. Gavin was strong and quick... and very, very aggressive. He actually enjoyed making sliding tackles on the AstroTurf even if it took his skin off. For Gavin, anything was worth it just to be able to crunch into a bone-shuddering tackle. He carried that slightly crazy streak off the field too. And I was his unwitting victim a couple of times when we'd stay in a hotel on an overnight trip. We were roommates and he would often leap off the top of the wardrobe onto my back as I entered the room after dinner!

I also struck up a good on-field strike partnership with Leroy Rosenior in the reserves. We were banging in goals and I was catching the eye of Jim Smith, our new manager. In just a couple of years I had seen three managers at QPR. Terry Venables was only at QPR for a month after I signed from school in 1984 before he went to manage Barcelona. Then the former England international and larger-than-life character, Alan Mullery, took over. I do remember being taken into Alan's office to meet him. As I entered the room I heard a voice through a haze of cigar smoke, 'So you're the best schoolboy in the country then?' 'Er, yes, boss!' was all I could stutter. 'Then prove it. Off you go!' I left the office without ever seeing his face – just the smoke. At that time, I was only setting out my stall at the club and didn't have much to do with first team things. But it didn't go that well for Mullery. He was sacked and, after an interim period when Frank Sibley took charge, in came Jim Smith from Oxford United.

My dad knew Jim. As Gillingham manager he'd played against Jim's teams before, and he highly respected him as a man and as a manager. 'One thing, Gavin,' he said, 'he loves to shout at players! But he really loves and knows the game of football.' I must admit, I was a bit nervous of Jim at first. He was a thickset northerner, who was, shall we say, 'follically challenged' and affectionately known in the game as the Bald Eagle. His speech emerged as a kind of growl, and he went red in the face as he berated you for losing possession of the ball in training. But Jim was a very good manager and was one of the game's great characters. He understood footballers, and he had a good sense about whether to drop someone or to bring someone into the first team. He also didn't mind taking a risk on a young player. Due to my good form in the reserves, he called me into his office one day after training.

'You're not far off the first team', he growled. I didn't know whether he was praising me or telling me off! But I was in the first team for my professional debut the following weekend. It was only days after my nineteenth birthday – Sheffield Wednesday at home.

***

This is it. The day has come. My first team debut. It's Saturday, November 29th 1986. I've just celebrated my nineteenth birthday eleven days earlier. I wake up. Dad's managing Gillingham. He's off to play a match up in the north of England. 'All the best son. You'll do well. I'll be listening for the result on the radio.' No internet. No mobile phones in those days. I eat my pre-match meal in the kitchen just as I remember my father doing so many Saturdays when he played for Charlton. Like father like son! I get dressed. Suit and tie. Mum and Lauren come with me as we make the drive from Barnehurst, Kent, to Shepherds Bush, London – the home of Queens Park Rangers FC. I've been at the club since I was a 15-year-old schoolboy. I've worked my way through youth and reserve teams. But this is where it counts. This is what it's for. The big league. I can feel that sensation of butterflies in my stomach as we arrive at the stadium. Fans are beginning to fill the streets outside. Programme sellers. Scarves. Hot dogs. The smell of burgers on the street corner.

We always feel we have an extra advantage with the AstroTurf as our home surface. We practise on the pitch itself every day during the week of a home match. We are familiar with the bounce and the extra speed with which the ball moves across the artificial grass. We practise for hours whipping crosses in, early and low, between opposing defenders and the goal: 'The Corridor of Uncertainty', we call it. These kind of crosses in that kind of area on this kind of pitch are a nightmare to defend against.

I'm playing wide-left in midfield today. Not my favourite position. But I'm just glad to be in the team. Jim Smith paces the dressing room as I get ready to go out for the warm-up. A bead of sweat forms above his top lip as he growls, 'Don't give the ball away. Don't give the ball away.' I am actually not worried about 'giving the ball away' until Jim starts growling. Now I am very worried! Everything is a blur. Soon I'm warming up with the lads. 'The Final Countdown' by Europe is playing over the Tannoy system. That's ominous, I think! The final countdown before the kick-off flies by. Shin pads on. Tie-ups secure. Encouraging words from striker, Gary Bannister, and captain, Terry Fenwick. The buzzer goes. A surge of masculine aggression amongst the players as we shout encouragement and make vows of victory. Out we go. Down the tunnel. The roar of the crowd as we emerge onto the pitch. Goosebumps. A few final stretches. The toss of the coin. We change ends. The referee's whistle. A crescendo of noise from the fans. The game kicks off.

The first thing I notice is the speed. I play on this surface all the time. But it's much quicker than training games or reserve team football. Lightning quick. Players think and move so much faster at this level. They execute difficult technique at top velocity. I need to be sharp. The ball comes to me: kill it dead at my feet! Pass it to a team-mate! A ripple of applause from the Loft End! A surge of adrenaline and confidence rushes through my veins! Nerves begin to settle.

The ball is played down the right wing. A whipped cross from flying winger, Wayne Fereday, right into that 'Corridor of Uncertainty'. I slip between two defenders. I know I have to dive to make contact. I get there ahead of my marker. I launch myself for a diving header. It skims off my head. Just past the post! I land and skin my hip on the plastic pitch. That's going to stick to the bed sheets tonight!

I run my legs off. Up and down the pitch. After seventy minutes I get cramp in both calves and I'm subbed to an ovation from the crowd: 2-2 is the final score. I did okay. 'Good debut, Gavin' says assistant manager, Frank Sibley, as I slip into a hot bath. The heat on my sore muscles feels good. The sense of satisfaction in my soul feels better. I've done it. I'm finally a first team player. I've made my professional debut. Like father like son! My mum and sister are waiting outside. I wonder if my dad knows the result.

***

Some people ask if being a Christian is compatible with playing competitive professional football. Can you be aggressive and ruthless with the opposition and show Christian love at the same time? Some managers and coaches have worried when one of their players has become a Christian because they fear the player will lose his edge. This wasn't the case for me. God had made me His and He also made me a footballer, just as He has placed many Christians in jobs in many different walks of life.

The Bible says that work is a good thing. God is a God who works in making all of creation, who works to sustain creation and who works to save His people. And a Christian is called to work hard with integrity, sacrifice and excellence in his or her workplace to reflect the goodness of God. There are rules to the game of football, and you must play hard within the rules with the aim of doing your best and winning the match. That means out-working, out-thinking and out-playing your opposition. Therefore, a Christian in any job should be the best kind of employee in their role.

Also, when I became a Christian, I became a better player simply because football fell into its right place in my life and I was a more rounded person. Currently much is being said about men's mental health issues in football and the broader society. Male depression and suicide are increasing across the Western world it seems. But when a man comes to faith in Jesus Christ, he gains a perspective on life and football that wasn't there before. Suddenly there is more to life. Football is great but it isn't everything. Football can be taken away from him, but Jesus Christ will never leave him. And suddenly the man becomes less frightened. No doubt there is a healthy fear to be had in football; a fear that can be beneficial; a fear of the unknown or of the consequence of defeat that keeps a player on his toes. But there is an unhealthy fear that paralyses and destroys, and many mental health issues are rooted in this kind of inordinate anxiety. But a Christian footballer realizes his identity is not tied to football. He is more than the sum of his performances on the field or trophies in the cabinet. By God's grace he is more than that and has hope beyond football and beyond this life. This is so freeing and fear-defeating. It's not that a Christian footballer can never have moments of depression or suffer in the ways above, but he knows where the lasting solution is found. Rather than looking inwards for help that will always fall short, rather than running to a bottle of alcohol or gambling or drugs for escape, rather than looking to end it all, he looks upwards to God for refuge – a God of love who never fails and gives hope to the hopeless. So being a Christian means having a whole new worldview which should make a man the best kind of footballer he can be. This is the truth, and this was my experience.

***

At the end of that debut season, in the summer of 1987, I was selected for England U/19s for a trip to South America – Brazil and Uruguay were the two destinations. Sir Bobby Robson, then England Senior Team Manager, was taking us. Bobby was a great coach, passionate about football and the honour of representing your country. His knowledge of the game was superb. His training sessions bristled with life. He instilled in us a pride in being England players. In that squad were, Paul Ince (West Ham), Paul Merson (Arsenal), Michael Thomas (Arsenal), David Hirst (Sheffield Wednesday), Neil Ruddock (Tottenham Hotspur) and others. It was an epic tour. Many of those players went on to have top class careers in the game. I'm sure, to a man, they all looked back on that trip with Sir Bobby as a true education and a privilege.

As great an experience as it was, this trip was nearly the scene of what would have been the most embarrassing moment in my career. We were playing Uruguay, and I was one of the substitutes that day. In the first half, Tottenham Hotspur's supremely talented midfielder, Vinny Samways, went down injured. 'Get warmed up Gavin', said Bobby Robson. I shot out of the dugout and started my warm-up along the touch line eagerly watching Vinny receive treatment from the physio, Fred Street, and selfishly hoping he would need to come off so I could get on the field for my country. That hope changed in an instant when I went to unzip my tracksuit top in preparation to take it off. Then I realized, 'Oh no. I forgot to put my England shirt on!' I was wearing the warm-up T-shirt. In seconds I could be called onto the field in an international match and wouldn't be able to enter because my jersey was in the dressing room. It would have been totally devastating and humiliating. Now my selfish hopes that Vinny would stay down injured and have to come off the field completely changed. 'Please get up Vinny!! Pleeeeaaase!' I repeated between gritted teeth. Thankfully he did. The half-time whistle blew shortly after and I sprinted for that dressing room before the others could arrive and quietly slipped into my England jersey. I had avoided what would have been – to my knowledge – an unprecedented blunder in international football. And no one ever knew. Until now!

I only came across Sir Bobby Robson a couple of times after that. Once was when I was playing for Newcastle United at St James' Park in a preseason friendly against Portuguese giants, Sporting Lisbon, whom Robson was managing. We won. I scored a diving header. I came out of the stadium at the same time as Bobby and just as the Sporting team were boarding the bus after the game.

'Hi, Bobby. Do you remember me from the U/19 South America trip?'

'Of course, Gavin.' He said in his lively Geordie accent. 'But tell me this. How does the smallest player on the pitch score a header against my team? See you, son!' And he got on the bus.

The second time I saw him was many years later in 2004, after I'd retired from playing football and I was doing some TV work for ESPN in Singapore. We were both analysts for the matches and worked for a week together. His insights were always better than mine. A man then in his seventies, having had a few battles with cancer he didn't quite have the energy of past years, and yet when it came to football, he became vibrant. At the end of one late night show, we were getting ready to leave the studio. It had been a marathon. Back to back matches. Bobby looked totally exhausted. Then I asked him a question about the game. He suddenly jumped up on a chair with all the energy of a teenager and began to explain his point. We shared a cab back to our respective hotels. He talked all the way home. Five years later he lost his life to cancer. That was Sir Bobby. Quirky. Courageous. Funny. Football mad. Admirable. Memorable. And lovable. A father figure to many players. I only wished I'd played for one of his club teams.

***

On the surface, things couldn't have been going any better for me. I was in the first team squad, playing for England U/19s and was handed a brand-new three-year contract by QPR. But I was in and out of the first team in those early days and admittedly a little impatient. I was also not being played in my best position. I could do a job at wide midfield or striker. But I wanted to be in the middle of the park – centre midfield with an attacking mandate. I had a good engine, could pass a ball and could get a goal. I figured that the 'goal-scoring midfielder' is what I wanted to be. That was my niche. But I needed to develop it at first team level.

In the autumn of that year, I was still living at home with my parents and my father was manager of Gillingham FC. Gillingham were doing well in the third division (today's

League One). He led them to the play-off semifinals only to lose marginally to Swindon Town in May 1987. Steve Bruce and Tony Cascarino had now left, snapped up by Norwich (Bruce) and Millwall (Cascarino). Nevertheless, my father still produced good teams that played good attacking football. Add to that an excellent coaching staff with Paul Taylor (from Columbus Magic), John Gorman (from Tampa Bay Rowdies) and chief scout Ted Buxton (from the Tampa Bay Rowdies backroom staff). Both Ted and John would be involved in future years with the England senior team under managers Terry Venables and Glenn Hoddle respectively. On a limited budget my father had turned Gillingham into a significant football club. The Kent club was on the football map, as it were. The fans loved him in the Medway area and to this day they still affectionately call him 'Sir Keith'.

One morning I came down for breakfast before making that long journey over to West London. Dad seemed distracted. Not his usual self. Then he said to me, 'I need a central midfielder and it occurs to me that there's one sitting at this table who could do a good job for Gillingham. Do you fancy coming on loan if Jim Smith agrees? Obviously, it's two divisions down but you can play regular first team football, which will be better than QPR reserves and I'll play you centre midfield. It will strengthen you.' And the decision to move to Gillingham FC was made over a bowl of Weetabix! My plan was unusual – to drop out of the top flight and go down a couple of divisions to gain valuable experience and then come back up to the top again. And so it was that I went from Loftus Road in West London to Priestfield Stadium in Kent, where I'd watched Gillingham many times in my father's tenure since returning from Tampa. Now, however, not only had I followed in my father's footsteps in becoming a professional footballer, I was playing for him. He was my boss! 'I cannot and will not show you any favouritism', he warned me. 'I'll be straight with you, Gavin. I will offer you less public praise than the others to avoid that perception. I'll give you two bad games then I'll drop you. But you'll do well here, and I believe your career will take off. You'll serve Gillingham Football Club well, and it will be your springboard to a higher level.'

It can be a tricky thing when your father is your manager. You need to be one of the team and yet you realize that sometimes they will moan about the boss in front of you, which can be awkward for everyone. It takes wisdom from both the father and son, and the son needs to be performing well on the field. I think he needs to be one of the best players in the squad to make it work. Otherwise the knives will come out early for both player and boss. But it can be done. It worked for Harry and Jamie Redknapp at AFC Bournemouth and also for Brian and Nigel Clough at Nottingham Forest. I always loved how the legend that was Brian Clough would always publicly refer to his son, Nigel, simply as, 'The Number 9'.

After a successful month on loan, my father bought me for forty thousand pounds from QPR, with a clause that gave Gillingham a percentage of any fee for which I was sold in the future. It was November of 1987. It was a risk. But I was determined to do my best for the club and my father and one day return to the top league. At least the whole family could go to match days together now!

5

NEW HORIZONS: MARRIED AND HEADING SOUTH

The first thing that struck me about Amanda Berry was her smile: attractive, bright, warm, and honest. She was late for history A level evening class that Tuesday in the autumn of 1986. This was shortly before my QPR first team debut. I had completed my English A level the year before and wanted to follow it with biology, but it didn't work with my schedule. History did. It wasn't my first choice, but it was the occasion where providentially I would meet the woman whom I would pursue to be my wife. We started chatting in the first break. 'What do you do?' she asked. I thought I had this one in the bag. 'I'm a professional footballer' is a sure-fire line to get the girl, isn't it? 'Oh,' she said, 'I don't really like football very much!' Needless to say, I was being humbled! However, she was interested when, as conversation proceeded, I told her I was a Christian. 'Come to church with me if you like', I said, and she agreed. That wasn't exactly my original planned offer for a scintillating date. Nevertheless, I went home later that night and prophetically wrote in my diary: 'Met a girl called Amanda tonight. Could get quite close to her.'

Amanda did come to Barnehurst Methodist Church with me and to the youth group; and after a while she too was won over by the good news about Jesus Christ. So, we began a friendship rooted in a mutual faith in God. She was working as a live-in nanny for a professional couple in London and over the next year or so we got to know each other well. I was drawn by her kindness and integrity of character. She was not only beautiful on the outside, more than that she was beautiful on the inside. We dated and very quickly I asked her to be my wife. After deciding to follow Jesus, this was the best decision of my life.

***

In those days Christians in Sport made contact with me through the National Director, Andrew Wingfield Digby. Andrew had been a first-class cricketer for Oxford and was the first paid employee of Christians in Sport. The organization began reaching out to Christians within the world of professional sport to support them and also to reach the world of sport with Christianity. Stuart Weir, Andrew's assistant, kept in touch regularly with me and through Stuart I was introduced to Graham Daniels.

Graham was a former professional footballer for Cambridge United, and had led one or two players to the Christian faith at the club in the mid-1980s. Graham also had the role of being the Christians in Sport evangelist back in those days. An enthusiastic and gifted communicator, Graham would speak about the Christian faith at universities all over the country. In addition, he began to connect with Christian professional footballers and would visit them over the football season to encourage them in their Christian walk, especially being someone who'd walked in their shoes (or boots!) before. Graham was a man who would become another hugely valuable personal friend and mentor.

I'd been at Gillingham almost a year by this time. I loved playing for my dad from the start. But our results were average.

After one 6-0 away defeat at Aldershot FC, things reached a head. I was useless on the pitch that night along with the rest of the team. And my father seemed particularly weighed down as we returned to the house together. The next morning, we were in for training at Priestfield Stadium. As I came through the door at the main ground, the club secretary told me my father wanted to see me in his office. His face looked grave. 'I'm letting you know I've been sacked. I'll be in the dressing room in a few minutes to tell the rest of the players. I'll see you in there.' I sat there in the dressing room that morning and watched my father and my boss tell us all he had been sacked. Everyone was stunned.

When a manager is sacked, it's never a pleasant thing and many people are affected: the man, his family, the players, the backroom staff, the fans. Sometimes it is a needed thing. A manager is in the results business and, if the results are consistently poor, his position can become untenable. Sometimes he loses the confidence of the players and that becomes a big problem. But sometimes sacking a man is a mistake. That was the case with my father, and it is not my judgement alone. To a man the players were devastated. The fans were outraged. The directors of Gillingham Football Club panicked after a few average results and one bad defeat. But we were still mid-table and in the third round of the FA Cup. No need to change things.

When my father returned to watch me play at Priestfield Stadium a few weeks later, the fans saw him walking up the main street to the stadium entrance and hoisted him on their shoulders carrying him all the way. My dad loved Gillingham. He had gained wide respect as a manager over the past six seasons by playing good football and developing players who were sold for decent money and who went on to do very well at the top level: Steve Bruce (Manchester United), Tony Cascarino

(Aston Villa, Chelsea) and Mickey Adams (Leeds United) to name three. They had been close to promotion the previous season, just missing out in the play-offs. Given more time he would have had the club promoted, I'm sure. But not many managers get enough time.

I was filled with mixed feelings at losing my dad as manager; unhappy with the directors, upset for my father, anxious for my own future. My father was crucial to the plan of developing me to be an established midfield player. I was still under contract and my immediate reaction after what the directors had done was to leave Gillingham. Paul Taylor took over the manager's position from my father. 'I want you to stay at the club, but I understand completely if you want to go, Gavin', he kindly offered. But I had come for a purpose, so in the end I decided to stay and attempt to complete it. Things didn't go well for the club after my dad left. It wasn't too long before another good man, Paul Taylor, was sacked. Next came Keith Burkinshaw. Here was someone who led Tottenham Hotspur to two consecutive FA Cup wins in 1981 and 1982 and then a UEFA Cup in 1984. I liked Keith very much. He was a gentleman. He was also highly experienced and respected, and he wanted to play good attractive football. But we simply didn't have the players to do it. He left after a few months and we finished my second season at the Gills relegated to the old fourth division.

I had been able to put in good performances, however. Somehow, I had found my groove, even playing in a struggling team, and in eighteen months had notched up over eighty appearances with a few goals to boot. Clubs like Walsall and Brian Clough's Nottingham Forest in Division Two (today's Championship, one below the Premiership) were showing interest in me. But it was AFC Bournemouth and a young Harry Redknapp who came up with £250,000 to make me their record signing to that date.

My dad and I met Harry in the Royal Bath hotel in Bournemouth, and the contract was sorted out very quickly. My father was my coach but also my agent. This was a huge help to me. Firstly, I knew he truly had my best interests at heart and wouldn't be swayed to encourage me to sign for a club because he got a better agent fee. Actually, he never received a penny from me. He did it because he was my dad. Secondly, in contract negotiations I could concentrate on speaking with the manager about football, tactics and my particular role, whilst my dad could narrow in on the hard end business talk. Thirdly, my dad knew all the managers I was ever involved with and had an instant rapport and trust with them. We worked well as a team in these meetings.

This was in June 1989. Meanwhile, a few months earlier Amanda and I had become engaged. We planned to get married in 1990. But when we knew my move to Bournemouth would mean me living over two hours from Kent on the south coast of England, we moved the wedding forward and on the 24th September 1989 Amanda Anne Berry and I were married at Barnehurst Methodist Church – the very same church where we became Christians and were members. We were both twenty-one years old. Here is the wedding weekend schedule:

Saturday 23rd September: Bournemouth *v* Blackburn. Scored my first goal for the club. Won 2-1. Drove back to Kent in the evening.

Sunday 24th September: Married Amanda. Reception at Dartford Football Club. Drove from Dartford, Kent halfway back to Bournemouth and stayed in a hotel just off the M3 motorway.

Monday 25th September: Drove from hotel to Bournemouth training ground where Amanda dropped me off.

Tuesday 26th September: Played Port Vale at home.

I don't think my new young wife could quite believe what kind of life she signed up for in marrying a footballer! Football the day before her wedding. Reception at the football clubhouse. Football training the morning after the wedding night. No honeymoon until nine months later…after the football season had finished. She knew I loved her more than football, but I was in a unique job that would take us on a fast ride for the next few years.

***

Life in Bournemouth was good for our early days of marriage. Though we loved each other deeply, we were navigating life together for the first time. Early on in our time on the South Coast, I came into contact with Tony Roake, a vicar at the local Anglican Church, St Andrews. Tony loved football. He had been an apprentice professional at Port Vale FC when he was younger and before he went into the ministry. He and his wife, Jill, took Amanda and me under their wings, as it were, and Tony began to teach me more about the Bible and marriage. We settled into the church over that year, and Tony and Jill became great friends. Tony remains a mentor to this day. I remember asking him about what it meant to be a leader in the church – a vicar or pastor or minister. He paused and reached into his pocket pulling out a small piece of towelling material and said:

> This is to remind me of the answer to that question, Gavin. On the night Jesus was betrayed at the Last Supper He took a towel and wrapped it around His waist and took the position of servant as He washed His disciples' feet. And when He rose to His feet that night there was no doubt in the room who the leader was. He was a servant king who came to die for the sins of His people and bring forgiveness and give them eternal

life in His kingdom. He laid down His life for His Bride the
Church – and you must do the same for your bride, Amanda.
That is the way a man must lead his wife. That is also the way
a pastor must lead his church.

In a few seconds he had shown me the nature of Jesus' leadership
– that true greatness is found in humility – and that I was
to be a Christlike leader to my wife: a pattern and example
I would hold before me from that day forward. In Tony and
Alan Fisher, the Bournemouth Club Chaplain, I was provided
with two older, experienced men who gave me wise spiritual
guidance. The book of Proverbs says: 'He who walks with the
wise will become wise, but the company of fools will suffer
harm' (Prov. 13:20). In other words, we are not born wise. We
need to become wise; and we learn wisdom from those who
are wiser, and usually a bit older. Sometimes in an age that has
idolized youth to some extent, we forget this principle.

The first year was good for our marriage. But it wasn't so
good for my football career. Harry Redknapp had assembled
a talented group of players at AFC Bournemouth, but we were
hit with injury after injury and never recovered well enough
to avoid the drop. Our final game of the season was against
promotion hopefuls Leeds United at home. It was a boiling hot
day on the south coast of England, and Leeds' fans had come to
celebrate and also to riot in Bournemouth. They beat us 1-0 in
the match due to a Lee Chapman header. They were promoted
to Division One, and we were relegated to Division Three.

It's remarkable to consider that after ninety minutes of
football against each other in the same division, two divisions
now separated us. And one year after signing from Gillingham
I was back down in the third division again. I remember
hearing the cheers and victory shouts coming from the Leeds
dressing room after the game and thinking, that must be some
feeling! My plan to go down a couple of leagues in order to

gain experience and to come back up to the top flight didn't seem to be working out too well. I was newly married, with a mortgage on a new house and all of a sudden, the financial and football future looked more uncertain. It happens that way very quickly in football. An injury or a relegation, and players who are already on short contracts are left in precarious positions. Being a professional footballer means living with uncertainty and constantly on the edge of big change.

Nevertheless, I'd played over fifty games that season and gained valuable experience. But I wanted to play at a higher level than Division Three so the first thing I did in the following week was ask Harry Redknapp for a transfer. Looking back, it was awful timing. Harry was feeling the pain of relegation more than anyone, and his record signing comes in and asks to leave a couple of days after the season finished. It was a selfish move on my part really. I should have waited and perhaps discussed things with him over the summer when things had calmed down and the rawness of relegation had eased.

That summer of 1990, however, proved to be hugely traumatic for Harry and Bournemouth Football Club in a deeper way than relegation. Harry and Brian Tiler, Bournemouth's Managing Director, went to the World Cup in Italy and were in a terrible car crash, which saw Brian lose his life. Harry was left in intensive care – life in the balance. It brought perspective back to everyone at the club as we were shown the brevity and fragility of life up close and personal. Suddenly relegation was not as big a deal as it seemed before. With his typical fighting spirit Harry recovered over the summer. I came back very fit and determined for the start of the next season, and we were enjoying life in Bournemouth having just bought our first house. I was playing well, scoring goals and catching the eye of a few higher division clubs.

And then the day came when my career really took a turn upwards. We were coming to the end of a normal training day. Out of the corner of my eye I spied Harry at the side of the pitch talking on his mobile phone and glancing over at me. The session ended and he walked directly towards me. 'Newcastle United have come in for you Gavin.' I heard nothing else. That's all I needed to hear. I went home to my wife and told her the news. 'Newcastle United have made an offer to buy me, Amanda!' She burst into tears as she looked around our quaint little three-bedroom semi-detached home. 'It's up north and it's cold', I continued. 'I know it would not be your first choice to move now. But it's a huge club, they are in the Second Division and this is the move I've been waiting for.'

Footballers wives have been portrayed in a negative light over the past twenty years – remember the hit UK TV show *Footballer's Wives*? In my playing era the term WAGs (Wives and Girlfriends) became a common descriptor for those married (or not) to the players. Certainly, at the top level of the game, wives have gained their own profile alongside their husbands. Of course, some came to the relationship with their own profile: think David Beckham and Victoria (Posh Spice). But when it comes down to it, footballers and their wives are ordinary human beings living in an extraordinary world – it's a goldfish bowl to some degree. Most don't get the attention that the Beckhams did and still do. But marriage to a professional footballer has its own unique challenges.

First, it is a transitory existence. My father was a one-club man and played in a time when that was unusual, but nowadays it is virtually unheard of. Ryan Giggs and Steve Gerrard are big exceptions that I can recall. We had sixteen different addresses over my eighteen-year playing career for seven clubs. That included hotels, rental houses and homes we bought. A footballer's wife lives with the constant thought that the two or three-year contract her husband signs might not even mean one year in one place. She knows the career is short (eighteen years is a long one), bad form or relegation cannot be predicted, and his job dictates where they live. Her job, if she has one, plays second fiddle to his.

My wife loved her job in Bournemouth working at a child development centre in Poole. But the instant I told her about Newcastle, she knew she would be leaving that job she so enjoyed and starting again in a different place. So, a footballer's wife must be adaptable, ready to make sacrifices, new friendships, get children settled into new schools, house hunt and make a new home in a new place very quickly. This skill, of course, is vital to her husband settling into his new club and playing well on the field. Add to this the fragile nature of her husband's job. He can be injured in one training session and lose his livelihood and the main source of income for the family. She might live with the privilege of above average income for a while, but she knows it's not for long. He's retired at thirty, maybe thirty-five if he has a long career. And not every professional footballer earns enough to live on for the rest of his life. Most don't.

Being the wife of a footballer also means living with a different mentality in the home. It's an intense job which means there is an intensity to the footballer's life. Diet is strict. You can't eat what you want all the time. Rest is crucial. A man in the office job might be up all night with the baby to give his wife a rest and as a consequence feel 10 per cent down the next day. That probably won't affect his job performance. For a footballer, that physical 10 per cent is everything – it might cost the team the game and him his place in the team. Many times, my wife made unseen sacrifices so I would be in optimum shape for match day. In addition, she knew that the job intrudes on all the public holiday times that most people enjoy at home. Easter and Christmas are major fixture times in the football calendar. Many Christmas Days were, at least in part, spent apart from the family, training or travelling to an away match to be played on Boxing Day.

The footballer's wife also lives with the reality of sharing her husband with the public. Public men get public criticism (not many wives have to sit through an afternoon of fans' abuse aimed at their husband) but also public adulation and attention. Her husband, whether playing for a Premier League team or a League Two team (four divisions below), is the focus of local and maybe national attention. She knows that fame may be addictive to him, but it is also attractive to others – male or female. They walk around with his name on their shirts. Men want to be her husband. Women might want to be with her husband.

Many nights Amanda and I went out for dinner and fans would come straight up to our table and ask for autographs, oblivious to the fact that this was our private time together. But these were the same fans that would wait for an hour and a half in the damp cold to get your autograph after a match on a Tuesday night away from home. One Newcastle fan told me that he could have paid his mortgage off years ago with all the money he'd spent following his team all over the country. That hit home with me. What does it cost to give an autograph and a bit of time to the people who make the game what it is? My wife was always gracious on those occasions when we were out together. We knew that these people also helped pay my wages, and there was a certain kind of glad obligation I felt towards them – even when the boundaries were stretched slightly!

Finally, a footballer's wife is married to someone who experiences an adrenaline rush in his job that few can match. Then he comes home to normal family life afterwards. How can she compete with that? She might live with the fear that football is more important to him than she is. Of course, aspects of these things are issues for any wife in any marriage. Transition, uncertainty, scrutiny, anxiety. But for the footballer's wife, these things are particularly intense and public in nature.

Knowing this, Amanda and I vowed to make our marriage our priority. Neither football nor anything else was allowed to take the place of each other. The Bible says that you become one flesh with your wife. There is no other human relationship that is closer. You are not even one flesh with your children. A mistake many husbands and wives make is that they have children and the children become the centre of the home. They forget to work on their marriage and then, when the kids leave home, the husband and wife are strangers. Marriage is a covenant – a promise made before God to commit for life to a person of the opposite sex. Sadly, in a day of quick no-fault divorces and the normalization of co-habitation, marriage is not valued as it ought to be. But football could never compete with Amanda in my heart and affections, and I am blessed that my marriage is standing long after football is gone. When you celebrate thirty years together, people are thrilled. Why? Because there is something deep down in human beings that says, 'Yes! This is good.' Love, commitment, forgiveness and faithfulness are things that few of us would deny are noble and to be desired.

When I broke the news about Newcastle United to her that day, we were in our first year of marriage with many trials and triumphs to come – things we couldn't even imagine then. Now we are past our thirtieth anniversary with much water under the bridge. But all we knew on that day in the autumn of 1990 was that Tyneside awaited us. So, within days we left Dean Court, the home of AFC Bournemouth, and headed to St James' Park, the home of Newcastle United. And we stepped onboard 'The Black and White Rollercoaster'.

6

THE BLACK AND WHITE ROLLERCOASTER

The first time I remember pulling on the black and white stripes of Newcastle United I was actually only six years old. Although my dad wore the red of Charlton Athletic, Newcastle blood flowed through our veins. My grandparents, Thomas and Lydia Peacock, were from South Shields in the North East and my grandad, Tom, grew up on a diet of watching football at St James' Park in the halcyon days of Jackie Milburn and Hughie Gallagher. I made a few trips to Tyne and Wear as a kid with my family to visit our relatives. One day we all had a big game of football on the local heath. I still have an old photo of me in my Newcastle kit, posing like a mini-professional player in the front row of a team made up of my cousins.

I don't think anyone was prouder than my grandad on the day I signed for his hometown club. He told me there and then, 'If you sweat blood for their team, the fans will forgive you many mistakes on the field. They need to see the club means as much to you as to them.' I never forgot that. Newcastle is a tough working-class area with a mining background. The football club is in the centre of the city and the place where the locals come to have their spirits lifted and hearts thrilled by their team. Newcastle United is called the Toon. The fans are the Toon Army. And they are as passionate as any in the world. There were days to come at St James' Park where the noise and emotion was like nothing I would experience again in league football.

Jim Smith, my former QPR manager, had taken the reigns at Newcastle a couple of seasons earlier. He'd kept an eye on my progress after I had left QPR and now wanted someone to give some energy and creativity to his midfield. After Newcastle United had agreed a transfer fee of £150,000 plus Newcastle winger Wayne Fereday (my old QPR team-mate) in exchange for me, my dad and I were invited to meet with Jim Smith, sort out contract details and then watch the team play at Nottingham Forest. Things went well with the negotiations: a three-year deal, a generous increase in salary and a good signing-on bonus. Moreover, Newcastle had just missed out on promotion the season before. They were in mid-table currently but had some experienced players like Scottish international captain Roy Aitken, goal-scoring machines Mick Quinn and Mark McGhee, and the inimitable John Burridge, a top goalkeeper and one of the great characters of the game.

After agreeing a deal and watching the Nottingham Forest game, I travelled back up to Tyneside with the team. I was to sign my contract the next morning at the stadium where I would be interviewed by reporters and the TV crews. It's always a difficult thing settling into a new club with new players, the banter, the in-jokes, the rivalries – plus you are hoping to displace someone from that team. But immediately I saw a familiar face as I got on the team bus that night in Nottingham. Mark Stimson had been with me at Gillingham a year before and we'd become friends. Mark and I played against each other as young professionals: he was at Tottenham Hotspur when I was at QPR. He always stood out as a very skilful left-footed defender, easily spotted by his mane of blond hair. He was a good player, but he also had a great love for the game and a keen eye for players. It was no surprise that after he retired from playing football he had a spell in league management for our old club Gillingham FC.

I arrived at the stadium the next morning ready to sign my contract. Ray Ranson, the veteran ex-Manchester City defender, gave me a tour of the stadium. He said, 'Just sign for this club. If it takes off here, it will be massive!' Next Jim Smith called me into his office. 'Gavin, the board think I offered you too much money last night. We'll still do a three-year deal, but it needs to be at a reduced salary. I'll step out for a few minutes and you think about it.' That was a curve ball and put a real dampener on things. Surely they knew what they were doing! Now with a young player in the office on his own – intimidated maybe – they probably thought I would just sign the reduced deal. I called my dad. No answer. Next I picked up the phone to the PFA (Professional Footballers Association). I spoke with Brendan Batson. Brendan told me to stand firm and insist on the agreed terms from the night before. I put the phone down and prayed. 'What do I do, God? You've opened a door here. I want to sign. But this is not right.' I remembered Ray Ranson's words, 'Just sign!'

Then it came to me. I called Brendan back, 'I'm going to sign for a reduced salary…but only for eighteen months, not three years. If I do well, I'll be renegotiating in a year for a way better deal.' Brendan wasn't convinced with my tactic. 'That's a big risk, Gavin. You may get injured. You may not play well. You're young and newly married. And you won't have the financial security of a longer contract behind you. I actually don't think they will go for it anyway. But all the best.'

I put the phone down and Jim came back into the office. I told him my terms. Without blinking he agreed, and the contract was signed. And the way things would go for me at

Newcastle, that contract was the best deal I ever did. Just like that, I was a Newcastle player. My Geordie relatives, Aunty Audrey and Uncle Michael, were warm and welcoming to us. Michael would often sit with Amanda at home matches. Aunty Judy and Uncle Jim had been in my life since I was a kid and their son, my cousin Simon who was a teenager at the time, would grow into an avid Toon fan during my playing days on Tyneside. He became the almanac of all things Newcastle United and is still to this day my go-to-guy for the latest news. With all my family surrounding us, Newcastle felt like home to us immediately.

My debut was at Leicester City a few days after signing my contract. I remember three things from that day. First, the thrill of seeing my black and white number 8 jersey hanging on the peg as I walked in the dressing room. Second, the noise of the multitude of fans that travelled to cheer us on that day and made it seem like a home game. And third, losing 4-3 after a Mick Quinn hat trick, but knowing I had a good debut and feeling immediately like this was the club for me. It was a big step up. There were players like Quinn, Ranson, Aitkin and Burridge that I could learn from, and I immediately began to settle in.

***

There is a great camaraderie amongst footballers and team-mates. So much so that even when you've not seen each other for years, it seems you pick up straight away from where you left off. You've done something very few people in the world get to do. You've experienced massive highs and lows together on the field where character is laid bare. You've sweated blood for each other, and that kind of bond stays with you. Then sometimes you make a friendship that goes way beyond the football field.

I found that with Mark Stimson. He and I, both being the same age and from the London area, palled up instantly; our wives were inseparable, and our friendship deepened. In fact, Mark and Julie were instrumental in helping Amanda and me settle so quickly in a new place. Mark was my best friend in football, and he and his wife Julie and their children Charlie, Chloe and Christie remain family friends to this day. Mark and I spent a lot of time together. We even had matching sponsored Rover cars. The lads nicknamed us after the hit detective series, Starsky and Hutch – I with my dark hair was Starsky (Paul Michael Glaser) and 'Stimmo', as we also called him, with his blond locks was Hutch (David Soul). Mark also tried to influence my clothes style. He was from London's East End and wore the cutting edge of fashion. I picked up a few tips from him and exchanged my old Puffa jacket for a sharp double-breasted Italian suit. Mark would always let me know if my clothes were sub-standard.

Not long after joining Newcastle, my mum bought me a winter sweater with a thick leather stripe running down the middle top to bottom – for the northern winter, you know. Mark hammered me every time I wore it to training! The 'my mum bought it for me' defence didn't stand up too well in a dressing room full of footballers with a pack mentality just waiting for someone to be the butt of the jokes that day (mainly so *they* wouldn't be the focus, of course). Years later when Mark had left Newcastle and was playing for Portsmouth FC, I wrapped up the sweater and sent it by post to him as a birthday present. After he recovered from laughing, he took it into the Portsmouth team dressing room and told them he'd brought in some new clothes from London's East End – the latest style in sweaters. One of their undiscerning Danish players actually bought it from him for thirty pounds. And my mum's sweater hilariously found another home.

But Stimmo's legacy in my life was more permanent than banter or fashion…it was baldness! We both had tremendous thick heads of hair back in the day. We had just left the 1980s after all. Then one day after training at Newcastle's Benwell practice ground, we were in the communal shower area.

'Stim, got any shampoo?' I asked.

'Yes. Get a look at this stuff, Gav. "Ice Blue Shampoo – Guaranteed to prevent baldness", it says it on the label.'

'That'll do me, mate!' I replied, as I grabbed it from him.

Within the next few years we were both losing our hair. Today, we both have exactly the same style on top – shaved heads. In jest, I always blame Mark Stimson for this because of the day he gave me Ice Blue Shampoo. Sometimes you can only trust your mates so far!!

***

Amanda and I rented a small apartment in historic Durham, a university city divided by the River Wear, with lanterns that lined cobbled streets, and a magnificent castle and cathedral that overlooked it all. It was like stepping back in time. Living there gave us a break from Newcastle itself where players couldn't walk down the street without being recognized. To give you an example, there was one day when Amanda and I went to the movies in Newcastle. As we were buying tickets, a big group of Newcastle fans spotted me and began to chant my name continuously until I went over and said hello. The vibe in Durham was a bit more laid back. Amanda loved it there. Life was good.

On the field I was playing well, but things were less than stable. I had arrived halfway through the 1990/91 season, and results were erratic to the point that Jim Smith was sacked only a couple of months after I joined. I was sad to see Jim leave. He was one of the really good managers in my era. He knew football well and had an eye for a player. He had a rough edge to him at times, but deep down there was an honesty about Jim. Plus, he cared about his players. He gave me my debut as a kid at QPR and as a mature player at Newcastle United. I will always be grateful to Jim Smith and the part he played in my career. He died in 2019 after a full life. And I can honestly say that The Bald Eagle certainly proved to be Gentleman Jim.

When a manager is sacked, it brings uncertainty to the whole football club even if everyone hopes the new man will do better. Players in particular get nervous. 'Will the new boss like me? Or will I be on my way out of here?' But the one who feels it most is the sacked manager and his family. The sack comes to most managers at some point. I knew the pain of it all after my dad was relieved of his duties at Gillingham a few years before. The public might say that the manager gets well paid, and maybe he does – certainly at top level clubs – but most managers you speak to feel the hurt of failure and public criticism when they are sacked. They aren't necessarily thinking about money.

Only weeks after I had signed for Newcastle United, Jim Smith left but the black and white rollercoaster continued. And in came Osvaldo Ardiles. Ossie, a former World Cup winner with Argentina in 1978, was a footballing legend. He'd already won the hearts of the British football fans during his time playing for Tottenham Hotspur and winning the FA Cup in 1980 with his unique style of midfield genius. He then headed into a successful management spell with Swindon Town before he arrived on Tyneside. Ossie was the kind of big name the club needed, and he played the kind of football that the fans wanted. He also loved to bring young players through. Players like Steve Watson, Lee Clark, Robbie Elliot and Steve Howey were all nurtured during Ardiles's time and progressed to become top players. After the first day of training he said to me, 'You are like a diamond that just needs a little polishing.' That was a boost. I mean Ossie had been Diego Maradona's mentor! I was no Maradona by any means, but if Ossie thought I was a good player and had potential to improve, that was good enough for me. He decided to play me at the head of his midfield diamond system, just behind the strikers. This released me into my best position as Ossie encouraged me to get forward and be creative. I blossomed and the goals began to flow.

After training, I practised my finishing for hours. Right foot. Left foot. Heading. Shots from outside of the box. Volleys. Half volleys. Shots from crosses. Shots from rebounds. One touch finish. Dribble and finish. I wanted to be able to take any kind of opportunity on match day and tuck it away. I loved scoring goals. I watched my team-mate Mick Quinn – a true Number 9. He was strong and single minded to the point of being quite selfish in the penalty box. All strikers have that about them to some degree. Their livelihood depends on it. So, I was a midfielder. But I developed the ruthless goal-scoring instincts of a striker. If I got a chance of shooting, I didn't panic and I was hungry to score. I would end up scoring 46 goals in 120 appearances for Newcastle United.

***

Goal scoring is its own art form. It's the most difficult thing in the game of football. It's the point of the game – to score more than the opposition. You can't win anything without scoring goals. That is why the goal-scorers usually get the best money and are a different breed in and of themselves. Goals are things of beauty, combining skill, balance, power and creativity in one moment on the pitch. Hours and hours of practice is aimed at that second or two which thrills the stadium. You can do all the passing, tackling and heading you want. But nothing will get the crowd on their feet or make them more vocal than a goal. In the first decade of the Premier League, it was a treat to watch supreme goal-scorers like Ian Wright (Arsenal), Alan Shearer (Blackburn and Newcastle), Andy Cole (Newcastle, Manchester United), Les Ferdinand (QPR, Newcastle, Tottenham Hotspur) Robbie Fowler (Liverpool) and Michael Owen (Liverpool) grace the Premier League. Each of them was magnificent in the art of putting the ball in the back of the net.

But I was a goal-scoring midfielder, and those kinds of players are very valuable to a team. If you have someone who can guarantee you eight to ten goals or more a season on top of your strikers' goal haul, it's gold dust. Scoring from midfield positions takes a knowledge of how the game will flow and an ability to see the big picture. It takes great fitness as you might make several lung bursting runs to get one chance. It also takes timing to make or hold your run so you arrive in space as the ball is delivered or breaks loose for you. Then it takes a cool head and sound technical ability to do the final thing and put that ball into the net. David Platt (Aston Villa and Arsenal) was exceptionally good in the 1990s. His record for the England national team was almost one goal in two games. Remarkable. But the man who emerged in the 2000s will, in my opinion, be hard to beat in the future anywhere in the world. That man is Chelsea's former manager and player, Frank Lampard. Frank was supreme in the particular art of scoring goals from midfield. His goal tally for Chelsea over fourteen years was a colossal 211, breaking Bobby Tambling's long-standing club record. It just won't be beaten.

One of the great privileges and delights of being a professional footballer is to be able to do something that lifts and delights people: something that brings them so much joy that they would pay to see it, and in many cases try to emulate it. Of course, there is personal joy in performing with excellence. But there is something wonderful about inspiring the next generation to be a footballer like you or giving hope to the city or town your club represents. Yet as a Christian there was another dimension to it all. All skill is given by God as a gift to be used for Him. To be a professional you need a certain amount of talent, for sure. But more than that, you need hard work, discipline, perseverance and wisdom. These are the character attributes that fan into flame the gift that all professionals have. They have excelled in these areas. Then once you make it as a professional you must continue to improve in order to fulfil your potential and stay at the top level. Staying there, riding the ups and downs and seeing off the competition year after year, is even harder than gaining that first contract.

Over the years I've heard people say two things repeatedly: One: 'I could have been a professional with a bit of luck.' And two: 'Footballers are not the smartest. They are a bit dim.' To the first statement I say, that is very unlikely. Maybe there is the small percentage that with better opportunity or better health could have made it. But most could not because they didn't have the base talent or the base character attributes above – mainly the character actually. To the second statement about footballers and their brains I say that maybe footballers don't have the book learning of many professionals in different walks of life or even like that of professional sportsmen like rugby players or American footballers and basketball players, who usually go to university before their sports careers. Football is more of a working-class sport – men leave school at sixteen (like me) and they don't get the chance to earn undergraduate degrees. But intelligence is not simply about passing exams. It's about common sense, wisdom to know how the world works, wisdom to know how to use your body in such a way and co-ordinate it at top speed that you dribble past two or three players; wisdom to read the game and intercept a pass from the opposition or make that goal-line clearance; wisdom to take a fifty-yard punt out of the air on one foot, transfer it in one movement to the other and hit it into the back of the net before the ball hits the ground. To do all this whilst others are attempting to stop you, the elements are against you and the crowd is cheering or jeering, takes great intelligence and wisdom.

But when you know that all skill is from God, true wisdom means diligently using and refining that skill in acknowledgement of God. The Bible says: 'The Fear of the Lord is the beginning of wisdom.' In other words, living life in reverence for and trust in the one true God is the start of living wisely. One of my heroes of the Christian faith is Eric Liddell. Liddell was a Scottish international rugby player and Olympic runner who went on to become a Christian missionary in China where he died in a prisoner of war camp during World War II. At the 1924 Olympic games in Paris he famously refused to compete in the 100m heats because they were held on a Sunday and Liddell was a strict Sabbatarian (he would not work or play sports on a Sunday because Sunday was set aside for God). He felt he must honour God before country. He stood firm on his principles in the face of national and international pressure on him to run. Then in a remarkable turn of events, instead of running in the 100m, he ran in the 400m final and won!

Eric Liddell was a man of great Christian conviction and integrity and his story was brought back into the public limelight in the iconic 1981 movie, *Chariots of Fire*. There is one moment in the movie that captures Liddell's understanding of how Christianity and sport relate. It comes where he is explaining to his sister, Jenny, how he must compete in the Olympics before he goes to China. He says, 'I believe God made me for a purpose – for China. But He also made me fast. And when I run, I feel His pleasure. To give it up would be to hold Him in contempt….To win is to honour Him.'

It was like that for me as a Christian footballer. To use my abilities well and win was to honour Him. And when I scored, and the crowd roared…I felt God's pleasure.

***

It was a real joy to play for Ossie Ardiles. Many of the younger players, including me, owe him a great deal because of the faith he showed in us. But we were poor defensively as a team and although we produced some great creative and attacking play, which the Toon Army loved, we conceded too many goals. Ossie lasted just about a year at the helm before he followed Jim Smith out of St James' Park. There were a few tears at the Benwell training ground on the day Ossie left the club. He was well loved by all – players and backroom staff alike. I travelled back to my house that day grateful for the past year with the little Argentinian but wondering who his replacement would be. I was driving my car over the Tyne Bridge when I heard the answer on Radio Newcastle. We had signed Kevin Keegan! 'Special K', as he was known on Tyneside, was returning to the Magpies with his assistant, Terry McDermott. And the club would never be the same again – neither would I.

Keegan had been one of football's first millionaires, able financially to retire at the end of his career. In fact, he finished his playing career at Newcastle United having spearheaded them to promotion and the top league in English football with a team featuring a young Chris Waddle and Peter Beardsley. They flew him off the pitch in a helicopter at the end of his final match at St James' Park, and Keegan and his wife moved to Marbella, on the Costa del Sol in Spain, where he played golf and tennis for seven years before that phone call beckoning him home to the North East of England. He says that he would have returned for no other club in the country.

'If any of you wants to leave this club, come and see me and I'll help you do so. But if you want to stay, we will survive this season and we will take off.' That was Keegan's opening line as he gathered the players together at his first training session. Keegan was a passionate and magnetic personality. He was 5' 6" tall but filled a room with his inspirational presence. And he was a true leader of men. As a player and captain for Liverpool, Hamburg, Southampton, Newcastle United and England, he was the kind who would inspire you by his example of giving everything for the team and using the talent he had to its best. When you couldn't give any more, Keegan would pick you up and carry you! That's true leadership – sacrificial and servant-hearted; brave and noble.

Kevin Keegan motivated players and he had the ability to know that what worked for one individual might be different for another. His first game in charge was against Bristol City FC at home. St James' Park was rocking and filled to the rafters with 30,000 Geordies. They were forced to lock 5,000 fans out of the stadium that day because capacity had been reached. The dressing room was tense. The manager had been with us only a few days. He had watched just a few videos of our team in the past few weeks, and so barely knew the players. As I was making final preparations – taping shin pads in place, tightening boot laces – I watched Keegan walk around the dressing room speaking to players individually: Liam O'Brien, David Kelly, Lee Clark. Then he came to me.

'You're the man today. You're the one! Bill Shankly used to say to me, "Just go out there and drop hand-grenades all over the pitch!" And I'm saying that to you. Just cause trouble wherever you go, and you'll win us the game. You're the man.' Bill Shankly was the famous Liverpool FC manager, who treated Keegan like a son when he played many successful years for them. 'Wow!', I thought, 'Shankly said that to Keegan.

Now Keegan, who was one of my boyhood heroes, is saying that to me!' I felt ten-foot-tall and burst out of that dressing room and down the tunnel. I felt like I could run all day, and I did. We won 3-0. Striker, David Kelly, scored two. I didn't score but played well and got a couple of assists. That kind of man-management marked Kevin. I always tell that story and inform people, 'Keegan is a great motivator of men!' A few years later when he took over as England manager, he won his debut match 3-0 against Poland at Wembley. Manchester United's midfield powerhouse, Paul Scholes, scored a hat trick. I remember picking up the newspaper the next day and reading Scholes's comments, 'Keegan is a great motivator of men!'

'That's right. I've been telling people that for years!' I thought to myself. Then I carried on reading Scholes's comments: 'He said to me in the dressing room before the game, "Bill Shankly used to say to me, 'Just go out there and drop hand grenades all over the pitch!'"' The exact same thing he said to me! And there I was thinking I was special!!! I laugh when I think of that, but the point remains true. Scholes was a goal-scoring midfield player and the type of character that Kevin knew would respond well to that particular encouragement. For other types of players and characters he used other tactics. Keegan was indeed a great motivator of men and Newcastle United were about to benefit from this.

To be a good leader you must be able to cast vision, have good man-management skills and hold both discipline and encouragement together in balance. If you say goodbye to discipline, you say hello to anarchy. But most people respond best mainly through encouragement. So, although discipline underpins everything, good leaders let encouragement be the lasting flavour. Kevin was an encourager, but he wasn't slack to confront you if you crossed him. He would say, 'I'll treat you like men and give you the freedoms of men, until you act like boys. Then you'll be treated like boys.'

Mick Quinn saw Kevin's tough side early on in his tenure. Quinn did an article about Kevin with the Sunday Sun and the headline read: 'Keegan's So Lucky If He Fell In The River Tyne He'd Come Up With A Salmon In His Mouth'. It was a bit disrespectful. Keegan was not impressed. He called Quinn into his office on Monday morning. Kevin just sat there facing Quinn with the article pinned to the noticeboard behind him. He never said a word about the article to Quinn. He just talked about the team and his plans for the next game, knowing that Quinn's gaze was constantly being drawn to that unfortunate headline nailed to the board. Quinn got the message, and it was clear from then on that he wasn't in Kevin's long-term plans. Kevin had him out of the club within six months.

Kevin knew he had been brought into a difficult situation. We were in a relegation fight. But leaders create momentum and change momentum. And good leaders love to surround themselves with other good leaders. They are not threatened by talent around them but use the talent to augment their leadership. That's true in all spheres of leadership. Too often I have seen leaders in sport, business or the church become very insecure when other strong leaders emerge around them. As long as the person is not trying to usurp the lead man, he can actually improve him. Kevin immediately brought in a big leader in Brian Kilcline. A huge fearsome defender with an even more fearsome beard that marked him out on the field, the former Coventry City captain and FA Cup winner was a brave captain and even though he was past his physical best, he was exactly what we needed to avoid relegation that year.

We had good and bad results under Kevin in his first few weeks. And our survival season went to the wire. In our penultimate game we beat Portsmouth at St James' Park due to a wonderful goal from my strike partner, David Kelly. But we went to Leicester City's Filbert Street for our final match still needing points to avoid the drop. Whether you are fighting for promotion or against relegation, the pressure at either end of the league table is immense as the season comes to a close. But it's way worse at the bottom. And I remember that day in early May 1992 as if it was yesterday....

***

'Lads, remember this. We will survive, and then this club will take off.'

These are Kevin Keegan's last words to us in the dressing room. There are almost 22,000 fans crammed into the stadium. The tension is at breaking point. It is unthinkable that, if we lose, we could take Newcastle United down into Division Three for the first time in the club's history. I look around at my team-mates, each one in his own world of thoughts; each one preparing himself to do his best; each one fighting his own doubts, battling to overcome them with positive thoughts. Nerves are palpable. I hear someone being sick in the toilet. But David Kelly looks confident. I like playing alongside him. He's fit, fast, strong in the air and very unselfish. We work well together. Ray Ranson, Kevin Brock, Brian Kilcline and Kevin Sheedy provide some much-needed experience for this occasion. As in life generally, experience is invaluable for pressure situations: those who have been there before know what to expect and can settle the nerves of the less experienced.

Out of the tunnel and into the arena we go. Like gladiators. Today, we live, or we die. The crowd literally explodes. The 5,000 Toon fans to the right-hand side drown out the Leicester faithful that surround and outnumber them. The Geordie faithful are magnificent. All I am thinking is, 'Give me the ball.' I feel like I will score. The whistle. Kick off. We start well.

Brock and I go close with efforts at goal. Franz Carr is looking lively floating from the right wing to the left wing. His twinkle-toed dribbling and rapid speed is frightening the Foxes. Before half time, our goalkeeper, Tommy Wright, punts the ball long up field. It's cleared by Leicester's giant defender and captain Steve Walsh, but only as far as one of his own midfielders, who stretches a foot to pass it backwards. It's a bad move. It goes past Walsh, but I've already seen it coming and I'm onto it in a flash.

Now it's just me versus the keeper, Carl Muggelton. But I know I will score. My heart rate drops. Things slow down in my mind. I feel in full control. I am aware of the noise and anticipation rising in the stadium, but it fades into the background. As the ball rolls towards the edge of the penalty box, I see Muggleton coming out to meet it. I know I can easily get there first. I will only need one touch to score. I check my stride and slow down slightly to lure him out and make him think he has a chance to get there before me. As we are about to come together, I pull my right leg back, but I prolong the backswing. That's key! The delayed backswing will tempt him, and he will dive in legs first. Then I'll be able to comfortably lift the ball over him. It happens exactly as I picture it in my mind that split second before. I clip the ball over the goalkeeper, leaving him helpless at my feet. I watch the ball roll into the back of the net and turn away to celebrate with David Kelly! First blood to us. Relief floods through the team.

But there's a long way to go. We hold that 1-0 scoreline until deep into the second half. We are getting nervous now. We've let leads slip many times this season. And we do it again…with only a minute or two remaining. After failing to clear our lines from a set piece against us, Leicester's big captain, Steve Walsh, rises high and powers home a header. 1-1! Confusion! Is a draw enough (1 point) or do we need to go for the win (3 points)?

'What do we do gaffer?!' I shout. Kevin Keegan and the rest of the bench aren't sure. Messages of other scorelines around the league are not filtering through yet. No time to talk. We kick off. The ball goes back to Tommy Wright. Another big punt up field. It's huge. It's a great kick. Walsh misses his header and the ball rolls on. Now I'm chasing the ball towards the Leicester goal – socks round my ankles – cramp gripping my calves. One last effort. Can I get there? Every fibre strains. Every stride I take is agony. Walsh is chasing behind me and lunges, a long leg getting there just before I can make contact with the ball. But as he does, he pokes it past his own goalkeeper! It hits the back of the net! It's in! We've won! We're staying up! And the sea of Newcastle fans to my left explodes with joy!

Like an avalanche the Leicester fans tumble onto the pitch from behind the goal. I start to bend my run away from them and towards the Newcastle fans in that far corner. But now the jubilant Toon Army pours onto the pitch as well – like lava from a volcano. They want to celebrate but also confront the Leicester fans that are now charging towards them. I'm stuck between them. There's going to be trouble. I feel trapped. I need to get off the pitch. We all do…and I'm the furthest away from the tunnel! I make my last run of the day, dodging past the masses as if invisible, football league safety in hand – now physical safety to be secured. I somehow make it through waves of fans and to our bench by the tunnel. I leap on young Steve Watson. Relief and euphoria together pump through my veins! The day is ours. Victory – saved from the jaws of defeat and relegation. Hope is on the horizon.

My grandad Tom isn't here. He's in hospital having just suffered a stroke. But I know he is here in spirit. A few days later I will go to visit him and give him my number 8 match shirt from that great day. He won't say much, but the tear in his eye will say it all. Three years after that moment another stroke will finally take his life. And my father will return that jersey to me and say, 'Your grandad loved this shirt. Till the day he died he never washed it because you sweated blood for his team on the day you saved them from relegation!' I will remember this day at Filbert Street for many things but none more than for honouring my grandad's words. I sweated blood for his team as he told me when I signed for them. My grandad was a special man, and I never think of him without feeling a surge of emotion and a surge of pride in my Geordie roots.

As Kevin Keegan predicted, we survived. Now the question is, can Special K deliver on the second half of his promise? Will we take off? The answer is yes, and I am about to experience the most emotional year of my life – both on and off the field.

**

Keegan and Terry McDermott signed new contracts and the first player signing of the new season was...me. That eighteen-month deal I'd signed for Jim Smith was at an end and had proven to be a shrewd decision. Things had gone very well for me on the field. I finished that season with twenty-one goals and now I had several teams who wanted to sign me. Chelsea's Ian Porterfield, Billy Bonds at West Ham, Glenn Hoddle at Swindon Town and Middlesbrough's Lennie Lawrence were all on the phone. But Kevin kept calling me into his office, offering me a better financial deal and telling me how Newcastle was the best place for me. One day I was in the sauna after training and all of a sudden Kevin's head appeared in the window. 'It's going to get a lot hotter round here!', he shouted through the glass, 'Sign the contract!' I think I always knew I would sign for Kevin. I loved playing for him, and I just believed he would take us up to the Premier League.

Keegan then signed former Everton and England defensive midfielder, Paul Bracewell, plus two skilful defenders in Barry

Venison and John Beresford. We were going to play football out from the back. Starting with the fullbacks. These players gave us a great platform to go forward. Then crafty winger Scott Sellars came in to take over from Kevin Sheedy, who was coming to the end of his career. I played up front with David Kelly, and the exciting Lee Clark played just behind us. Our movement and football were unstoppable, and we started the season like a steam train destroying everything in our path. We played some of the best football I ever experienced in my career. Then Keegan played a masterstroke and signed Robert Lee from Charlton Athletic.

Actually, I recommended Rob to Kevin. My father, Keith, was by then a coach at Charlton and knew Rob was coming to the end of his contract and looking for a move, with Charlton willing to sell for the right price. Rob was talking to West Ham, the club he supported as a boy. Keegan didn't know much about him. But I remember saying to Kevin, 'Get Lee if you can. He's a top-class player.' Keegan sorted out a meeting. He was such a powerful and persuasive character and he really sold the club to Rob. Lennie Lawrence at Middlesbrough was also wooing him, but Keegan told Rob that I had turned down 'Boro because Newcastle was the bigger and better club. Knowing he was a London lad and would want to get home regularly to visit his family, he also told him that Newcastle was further south and closer to London than Middlesbrough. It wasn't true of course (Newcastle is north of Middlesbrough), but Rob believed him and the combination of Keegan's hard sell and Rob's bad geography led us to the acquisition of a player whom Keegan would describe as his 'best pound for pound signing' and someone who would become, in my opinion, one of the best midfielders in Newcastle's history!

Rob was an intelligent and versatile player who added another dimension to our team. With him in the ranks we continued our run of victories. We won the first eleven games of that season – a club record – and accelerated to the top of the league. Now, instead of feeling apprehensive about the next game we were about to play, we couldn't wait for Saturday. We also had a good team spirit. The addition of strong characters like Venison and Bracewell meant that the standard in training sessions went up. The players began to demand excellence from each other. Everyone wanted to win, even if it was the Friday five-a-side. We trained hard, and so we played hard in matches, taking that high standard with us.

The best football teams I played in were the ones in which each player was placed in his best position within the team. Each person had a specific role. I remember Keegan, sitting me down in his office one day and showing me our team on a tactics board. 'Just look at my team', he said. 'When the goalie gets it, he throws it to the fullback. The centre backs drop deep, one midfielder shows for the ball, one winger stays wide, and one striker comes deep whilst the other one runs in behind the opposition defence. Look how we fit together and move up the field. We are so fluid.' He was painting a picture of a machine he was building on the football pitch. The point was, everyone knew their position and fulfilled their role in that machine. And this well-oiled machine won promotion to the Premier League that season. There was order and harmony. Everyone knew his purpose. Keegan had the knack of being able to get individuals to win together.

Even though Brian Kilcline was club captain, I was made team captain early that season. I remember doing an interview for the local paper about my captaincy and also my Christian faith. To my dismay the headline came out: 'Why I Can Never Be One of the Lads'. As soon as I saw it, I thought, Oh, no! This won't go down well in the dressing room. I had no control over the headline, and I had not meant it to come across as separatist or elitist, just that as a Christian I do live with a different mindset than those players who are not. I don't think Barry Venison thought much of that article. He had some harsh words for me from then on at different times over the season. Maybe he thought he should have been captain (after I left the club he was). Maybe he didn't like my public Christian stance. Not every player you play with is necessarily your cup of tea, but good players and decent men set that aside or sort out personal differences for the sake of the team.

As I look back, I should have done more as captain to win over the likes of Venison and Bracewell. After all they were champions and had done way more than I in the game. I could have sought out their wisdom on how I ought to handle the captaincy of Newcastle United. I was a young captain who led by example, who could inspire my team with a goal or assist and who was vocal on the pitch. But I lacked something that Keegan pointed out to me one day, 'As a captain you need to give even more of yourself to the team than the other players.' They were wise words. I captained Chelsea and QPR after Newcastle, and I grew into this wisdom in my latter years as a captain at QPR. Captaining my teams was one of the great honours and privileges of my career.

***

Meanwhile we were running away with the league. David Kelly and I were smashing in goals of all types, Lee Clark was running teams ragged and Rob Lee got better with each game. I was learning from Kevin Keegan. We all were. He spent time working with us individually; he taught me how to get into positions and score more with my head even as a small guy. He also taught me how to be wise and intelligent in the battle.

'Don't try and wrestle physically with big defenders. You might be strong but they are stronger. Keep the ball moving when it comes to you and take the defenders where they don't want to go', he would say.

So, I would come deep into midfield positions. And Clark would run in behind. The defenders didn't know whether to stay with me or go with Clark and we created so much space for each other. I also ran them into the channels out wide. They hated it. But I was completely comfortable in those spaces and, because of my stamina, I could do it all game long.

Our players were also getting noticed in wider circles. Some were even getting international call-ups. A personal highlight for me was being selected for a league representative team that faced an Italian representative team in a mid-season exhibition match. We were coached by Glenn Hoddle (then Swindon Town manager). I was awarded man of the match by former Italian World Cup winner Marco Tardelli, and my performance also secured Glenn's personal interest in me as a player.

Newcastle United was now a free moving, free scoring unit, beautiful on the eye and playing mouthwatering football that the Toon fans loved. But after an incredible first half of the season, by February we were struggling to maintain our momentum and freshness. Keegan knew he needed to do something to change this, so he took us for a mid-season break to Marbella in Spain – his old stomping ground. We went to train there for a few days away from the cold, northern English winter. The idea – to build some more team spirit and recharge for the final run in. One evening Kevin took us all out to the famous oceanfront Italian restaurant called Tony Dalli's. The food was great, and Tony would croon out the old Italian classics including a bit of Frank Sinatra.

That night the players and coaching staff were sitting at a long table looking out at the ocean, when in walked the world-famous actor, Sean Connery. He strolled over to Kevin and gave him a hug. Sean and Kevin were friends and had played golf together regularly during Kevin's seven-year Costa del Sol sabbatical. They exchanged a few words and then Connery turned to us. 'How are you doing, lads?', he said with that famous Scottish brogue. 'You better not spend too long on the beach or else you won't get promotion! Make sure you finish the job. I know you will.' We were all left choking on our pasta. I mean, James Bond had just been at our table and given us a team talk!

Marbella was just the tonic we needed. Our league form picked up as soon as we returned, and with the signing of Andy Cole's goal-power from Bristol City FC in the transfer window, we went on to comfortably win the league Division Two championship and gain promotion to the Premier League. I scored eighteen goals that season but sadly missed most of the last few weeks with a hamstring injury. I got fit for the final two games but was on the bench. In truth we technically won promotion in our penultimate game at Grimsby – a great night it was. Then the final game was Leicester at home. And it was celebration time. What a difference a year had made when we had been fighting for survival against that team twelve months earlier.

We beat them 7-1 at St James' Park that day. I came on from the bench in the second half. It was a carnival atmosphere as I paraded with my team-mates around the stadium at the end of the match –Queen's 'We Are The Champions' blaring out. Our big Czech Republic goalkeeper, Pavel Srnicek, who had arrived at the club in the same week I did, famously pulled off his keeper jersey to reveal a T-shirt with 'Pavel is a Geordie' written across it. It remains an iconic moment in Newcastle United history. Pav and I roomed together for a while and got to know each other quite well. He was a gentleman, a kind man with that elusive virtue…humility. This is why he endeared himself to everyone. He never thought too highly of himself. And this is also why he learned to become a very good goalkeeper. I was so saddened to hear of his early death in 2015 at the age of forty-seven. To team-mates, coaches and fans alike, the big man with a humble heart will always remain – 'Pav the Geordie'. Back then for Pavel and the rest of us, the Premier League beckoned. But little did I know that Leicester City, the team I made my Newcastle debut against in 1990 and the one I scored my most important Newcastle goal against to keep us up in 1992, would turn out to be the last team I would play against in a Newcastle jersey in 1993. Amanda had fallen pregnant with our first child in the September of 1992. Nine months on and she was due to give birth right at the end of the season: an event that would direct us back down to London.

***

The week after the final game at St James' Park we ride in an open-top bus to display the Division One championship trophy and celebrate with a hundred thousand ecstatic Geordies who line the pavements of their beloved city. As I survey the scene below, I am at the height of my career so far – captain of Newcastle, a lucrative contract in hand, and yet still young and at the peak of my physical powers. Amanda is there with the other wives. It seems that her pregnancy has fitted perfectly in line with this season – from early season excitement and the first flutter of movement in her belly, to mid-season endurance and discomfort as life within her grew, to the end of season anticipation of glory and joy as our baby inside her seemed to kick every ball at the Leicester match. Life is great. And I can't wait for the birth. It will be the icing on the cake of a tremendous year. I give thanks to God for all His blessings.

A few days later and we are at the hospital. Amanda is in labour. I call our parents. They will be here in a day or so. This will be the first baby in our families for over twenty years.

Team-mates and wives have been wishing us well. Mark and Julie Stimson have been with us all the way. The press knows about the pregnancy too, and journalists who have become friends in my time at the club are keen to hear whether it's a boy or a girl. Everyone is excited. But the labour is hard and long. Twenty-four hours later and Amanda is still in great pain and the baby won't come. The specialist is brought in. He gives her an epidural injection. She's slowly losing strength and becoming exhausted. So hard to watch. I can't help my wife – I can only encourage. They are concerned that the baby isn't getting enough oxygen. They use probes to take blood from the top of the head to check the oxygen levels. Excitement has now turned to anxiety. I call Tony and Jill Roake. Prayers of thanks have turned to prayers for help.

Parents arrive from the south of England – labour has taken that long! Amanda battles on. She's a fighter. But she's losing energy. After forty-eight hours the specialist finally uses forceps to deliver our child. The cord is wrapped twice around the neck. They deal with it quickly. I am by my wife's side and look to see if it's a boy or girl. A boy! At last! Euphoria! Fear is replaced by joy. But now he cries and puts his arms out to the side. Something's not right. He has only one hand. Half of his right arm is missing. My stomach turns over. The shock is huge. Amanda sees it on my face. 'What's wrong?' she says. 'His arm. He doesn't have his right hand', I quickly reply.

Nurses take him aside. Talking. Concern in their eyes. There is a delay, which seems like forever. I look at my wife. Tears are in her eyes. I feel sick. Confused. The ground feels like it is moving beneath me. The specialist comes back to us.

'Gavin, Amanda, in one in ten thousand pregnancies a thread of the amniotic sack can come away and wrap around where a limb would grow. It can simply stop blood supply and prevent growth. It's called an amniotic band. It probably didn't show on your scan because of the way he may have been lying on that day.' (We only had one scan in those days). 'Do you have a name for your baby?'

'Jake', we say.

'Listen to me. I've seen this before', he continues. 'He will be okay. This is the body God has given little Jake.'

Instantly the sovereignty of God is spoken into our lives as tears roll down our cheeks. Yes. God is still in control. I don't know why He chose things this way, but He is good and wise. I know this because He gave His own son, Jesus, for me. The ground beneath me begins to firm up again. But the pain remains. The nurse hands Jake to my wife. She looks at him with instant motherly love. God has given her remarkable fortitude and he has given me a remarkable wife. In God's providence she had worked with a little boy with exactly the same limb deficiency at her child development centre job in Bournemouth. It's as if He was preparing her for this moment now. Now it's my turn to hold him. I looked at the bundled up little body in my hands – I'm suddenly so aware of my hands. Two dark brown eyes stare back up at me from below a mop of spiky black hair. I have a son. My mind races on. Are there going to be other health issues related to this? Will he be able to do everything he needs to do? I'm filled with love and a fatherly sense of protection. But my heart is breaking. Football isn't even in my mind anymore.

***

It's hard to describe the mixture of pain and joy in that moment. But that's how suffering works. Everyone suffers to different degrees. Many of you reading this, if not all, will be suffering or will have suffered multiple things in your life: sickness, death of loved ones, financial worries, relational strife, physical and mental abuse. Suffering means loss or denial of something. To put it in reverse terms, it means taking on an uncomfortable experience. Suffering hurts us, suffering confuses us, suffering exhausts us. We live in a suffering and broken world. That's plain to see: a world of war, poverty, tyranny and terrorism. Dysfunction is everywhere. In my and Amanda's own moment of acute suffering, I remember God's promise of a world with no more suffering for His people.

'He will wipe away every tear from their eyes, and death shall be no more, neither shall there be mourning, nor crying, nor pain anymore, for the former things have passed away' (Rev. 21:4). That's one of the great things about being a Christian. You are not immune to suffering or the pain it brings, you don't always know why it happens, but you do know the God who is in control despite the trial of the hour and you know He is good and merciful. And this God promises heaven and no more suffering for all who trust in His son, Jesus, for their salvation.

***

My mind turns to my father and mother, Keith and Lesley, and to Amanda's mum, Mary, who are all anxiously waiting in another hospital room. I leave the delivery room, gather myself together and pray for strength to be strong for them as I enter the waiting room. 'It's a boy.' Their faces light up. 'But there is an issue with his arm', I continue. 'He is missing his right hand.' There are tears and hugs as I explain what happened. They come in and hold their first grandchild and love him instantly as they will do with all their grandchildren to come. They are rock solid in their support of us all.

The nurses take Jake overnight. Football doesn't matter to me at this point. I don't really care if I play again. I would give it all up for my son to have his other hand. I am twenty-five years old. At the peak of my powers I have been brought to the end of

A mother's love can never be broken. My caring mum has always given me her all.

My mum and dad, Keith and Lesley, getting married in 1965. Dad looks sharp, mum looks stunning. They both look like they mean business!

No one could get the ball off me when I was a Charlton mascot!

Geordie roots! Wearing the black and white stripes early – with my cousins on a family holiday in South Shields.

Like father, like son! I always looked up to my dad. I still do. A wonderful role model who gave me so much. Here we are in Tampa, Florida wearing the shirts of two football legends, who played in the NASL (North American Soccer League) when my father was assistant coach of the Tampa Bay Rowdies in 1980.

Rising stars! Epic England U19 South America tour in 1987 under Sir Bobby Robson. Left to right standing: B. Horne, G. Peacock, D. Hirst, J. Polston, M. Thomas, P. Ince, N. Ruddock, B. Robson, S. Redmond, F. Street, D. Howe. Left to right front row: V. Samways, R. Harvey, P. Moulden.

Young guns! Gavin Maguire, Justin Channing and I all came through the QPR youth system.

Head down – eye on the ball! Scoring for the Gills at Priestfield Stadium in 1988. My dad had bought me for forty thousand pounds from QPR a year earlier. The club then sold me in 1989 for two hundred and fifty thousand pounds to Harry Redknapp's AFC Bournemouth – a record fee for both teams at the time.

A spell on the South Coast. Playing for AFC Bournemouth in 1989 against Newcastle. Here I am tackling ex-Gillingham teammate and good friend, Mark Stimson. We would be together again in 1990, when I signed for the Magpies.

Marrying my one true love, Amanda, in 1989. After following Jesus, this is the best decision I ever made.

Howay the Lads! Ball at my feet, the Toon army behind me – and the goals flowed. When I signed for the Magpies in 1990, my Geordie grandad Tom told me, 'If you sweat blood for their team, the fans will forgive you many mistakes on the field'.

Premier League here we come! Just won the First Division Championship with Newcastle United in 1993. Kevin Keegan turned us into a free moving goalscoring machine, playing some of the best football I ever experienced.

Left: Pure Genius! I learned so much from my Chelsea boss, Glenn Hoddle: one of the most gifted minds as player and manager in world football. You gotta love those 1990s shell suits... or not!

'The Mighty Midgets': Mark Stein, John Spencer, Dennis Wise and I caused many Premier League defences a problem in the mid 90s.

Four generations of Peacocks: With my beloved newborn son, Jake, my father, Keith, and my late Grandad, Tom. (Jake is now a professional Muay Thai fighter and owns his own gym in Calgary, Alberta.)

Above: Doing the double over United! Scoring the winner in a 1-0 victory at Manchester United in 1994. I also scored the winner in the same scoreline at Stamford Bridge earlier that season.

Left: Wembley joy! The first of my two goals in a 2-0 FA Cup semi final victory against Luton Town in 1994.

When we were young. Happy times with Amanda, Jake and Ava.

Loving life at Loftus Road! I walked into the stadium as a starry-eyed 15-year-old schoolboy. I went on to play more than 200 games and score over 40 goals for this great club.

Always a thrill to score for QPR at the beloved Loft End (Richard Langley closes in to congratulate me!) I started and finished my career playing for the SuperHoops – a spell of ten years.

Valley Boys! I finally got to put on the red jersey and play for Charlton in the Premier League, albeit too briefly. My dad and I are the only father and son to have both played for the Addicks.

A pundit's life! Commentating on Portsmouth v Bolton Wanderers in the Premier League in 2006 – with BBC's king of commentary, John Motson, to my right and Simon Brotherton to my left. Bolton manager 'Big Sam' (Allardyce) looks down from above.

Just before leaving the UK for Canada in 2008. Back row (left to right): Jake, my sister Lauren, me, Amanda. Middle row: My niece Shania, Ava, my brother-in-law Andy and my niece Celine. Front row (seated): my father Keith and mother Lesley.

Preaching the Word at Calvary Grace Church.

Proper cold in Canada. My mother-in-law Mary with Amanda and me in minus 20 degrees!

Daddy's girl! Walking my beautiful daughter Ava down the aisle.

A family portrait: Austin, Ava, me, Amanda, Christa and Jake. My role as a husband and father has been the most important and fulfilling vocation of all.

myself. And I realize you are never really in control of your life. Because of the circumstances, I am allowed to stay in Amanda's hospital room that night on a put-up bed. We pray briefly. We collapse exhausted. Hearts are aching. But God's mercies are new every morning. They will be there for us tomorrow.

***

The next week consisted of a battery of tests and X-rays for little Jake, and visits from family and friends, one of whom bought him a 'Geordie Passport'. It read inside: 'He's Jake the Geordie now!' Every day and every test brought better news. It is amazing how grateful you can be that your baby is only missing a hand. The press was constantly calling for updates and wanting to speak with me. However, one national newspaper did their own thing and printed a small piece saying Jake had brain damage. This wrong information caused a lot of unnecessary problems and pressure as friends whom we hadn't yet been able to contact were anxiously calling us on the phone. My dad was an immense help as a buffer for me with the media. But it was now clear that the birth of our new baby and the complications therein were suddenly no longer a private affair.

And then all of a sudden, we began to receive letters of encouragement from all over the UK. Parents who had children with similar conditions to Jake told us that their children lacked nothing and were thriving. Adults with one hand inspired us with their stories of bravery in the face of adversity. We even received one letter from a highly talented one-handed golfer. Kevin Keegan was also wonderful to us. He kept in regular contact with me. He was concerned for Jake and for Amanda. After a couple of weeks, I went to see him. 'Boss, I know it's early days, but I think my wife and I would like to return to London to be near our families. We are new parents and we have extra challenges here. I love Newcastle, but I think this is more important.' Kevin's reply was straightforward, 'I don't want you to leave. I'm selling David Kelly. I'm bringing in Peter Beardsley. I think you, Cole and Clark can play well with him. But if your wife is not happy then you will not be happy, and you won't play your best football. I'd love you to change your mind, but if you want to leave, I won't out price you in the marketplace.'

Kevin Keegan was very gracious and showed a compassionate side that served his excellent man management. Being a winner doesn't preclude this. Many winners have a ruthless side to them that doesn't allow for compassion, but I don't think it needs to be so. Bill Shankly, Keegan's mentor, famously once said, 'Some people think football is a matter of life and death. I assure you, it's much more serious than that.' I think there may have been a twinkle in his eye when he said this. But what Keegan displayed in the way he dealt with my situation was that there were other things that superseded the beautiful game. Within a few weeks the phone call came. 'Hello, Gavin. It's Glenn Hoddle. I'd like to make you my first major signing at Chelsea Football Club.' It didn't take me long to say, 'Yes.' A fee of £1.25 million was struck between the clubs – a significant price. Alan Shearer had only just smashed the British transfer record in 1992 with a £3.6 million move to Blackburn FC from Southampton FC. Three years earlier I had arrived at St James' Park for a fee of £150,000 plus Wayne Fereday in 1990. Three years later I left, making a good profit for the club.

So, with a tear in my eye, I ended my ride on the black and white rollercoaster. There were certainly highs and lows and even at the height of success there was a bitter sweetness to it all. I had done well for Newcastle and had become a better player in my time there with 46 goals in 120 league and cup appearances – many of those in midfield.

I knew I would miss the fans, many of whom had become friends. Like John Shearer, known to all as 'Elvis'. I would give him a ticket for home matches and he would wait for me before and after each game just to carry my bag to the car and say hello. His name will not make the history books, but it is thousands of unknown people like him who make Newcastle United so special.

So truthfully, the honour was mine. From the moment I wore my Newcastle shirt as a little kid I was destined to play for the club. Now I would never pull on that famous shirt again. But to be part of the history of this special club was my privilege, and something inside me will always love Newcastle United Football Club and the people of the Toon. But then again, of course I will – Newcastle is literally in my blood.

In life timing is key. A year before, Glenn had wanted to sign me when he was manager at Swindon Town. But there were things for me to achieve on Tyneside. Glenn had won promotion with Swindon. John Gorman, my father's old team-mate at the Tampa Bay Rowdies and Glenn's great friend, had taken charge there. Now Glenn was at Chelsea and set to spearhead a King's Road Revolution! Therefore, in the summer of 1993, Amanda and I packed up house once more, and with baby Jake in tow we headed south – this time for West London and Stamford Bridge, the home of Chelsea FC.

7

THE KING'S ROAD REVOLUTION

Kevin Keegan said two things to me before I left the North East. First, 'You will learn more from playing with Glenn Hoddle in training than anything else.' And second, 'You are leaving one big club and joining another.' Kevin was correct on both counts. Glenn was thirty-six years old and a player-manager. He positioned himself as sweeper in the middle of three central defenders with wing backs either side getting forward. He had won Swindon promotion with this system the season before. I played as one of three in midfield with Dennis Wise and Eddie Newton. Eddie held the centre whilst Dennis and I had freedom either side to join the two forwards. It suited me perfectly. The beauty of the system was that you could move from five in defence to five in midfield in a flash. Wing backs were key as they gave us width. But Dennis and I were also able to deliver good crosses when we got into wide areas. And when Glenn moved into midfield from sweeper, he was devastating.

I had never played with any other player who had a mind quite like his. He had no speed, was not a great tackler nor was he powerful in the air. But he owned the football and it did whatever he wanted. As we say in the game, 'he made the ball talk'. When Glenn had it at his feet, things happened. As soon as he was on the ball, I would make a run. I didn't even need to look because I'd literally hear the ball whistling over my head with just the right spin so that it landed in my path at just the right speed.

Chelsea was a big club – though it had lost its way somewhat. It was an attractive club even before the big money and big trophies came along. Situated in the famous, expensive and highly fashionable King's Road, the club had been graced by supreme talents like Peter Osgood, Charlie Cooke and Alan Hudson. The Chelsea boys had swagger on and off the field and were a draw even for Hollywood movie stars like Raquel Welch photographed in the Chelsea kit (apparently she loved the blue!) after she came to watch a match at Stamford Bridge. After one match Steve McQueen even popped into the dressing room to say 'Hi'. Peter Osgood was without doubt the biggest star of that era and a larger-than-life character. He stood over six feet tall and had a rare combination of power and grace that tortured defences as he scored goal after goal. I did a few hospitality days with Peter at Chelsea in the early 2000s and really enjoyed hearing his wisdom on the game. Sadly, in 2006, he was another who died of a heart attack at a relatively young age.

However, for all its fame and glamour, by the time I joined Chelsea it had been a long time since significant on-field success had come to the King's Road. The mid-'80s saw Kerry Dixon, David Speedie and Pat Nevin helping to establish Chelsea back in the top flight after a spell in Division Two. But now the First Division had become the Premier League and as a new era was dawning for the game of football, so it was for Chelsea Football Club too. Glenn was a visionary on the field as a player but also off the field as a manager. He had spent time as a player with Monaco after being a one-club man for Tottenham Hotspur all his life. At Monaco he came under the coaching of a young

Arsene Wenger – the future Arsenal manager – from whom he learned much. In that way he brought a continental way of thinking to Chelsea. His predecessors, Ian Porterfield and then briefly David Webb, had a physical approach to the game, but Glenn wanted to play football out from the back and on the ground.

Glenn also changed the players' lifestyles. When I arrived at Chelsea, we used to have tea and biscuits in the dressing room after training. There was actually a biscuit rota! Dennis Wise, the captain, was the enforcer. If it was your day to buy the supply, you would likely get a phone call from 'Wisey' on the way into training, 'Oi, Peacock, make sure you buy some good biscuits, expensive ones, or you'll be on double duty.' It didn't take Glenn long to ban the biscuits and bring in a chef. It became compulsory to stay for lunch so you could refuel your body properly. Football clubs were making use of the progress in sports science. We hired a kit man and masseur in Terry Byrne. We also employed dieticians and even Ian, the reflexologist. Ian used the ancient Chinese art of manipulating pressure points on the soles of the feet, which supposedly stimulate muscles and major organs in the body. We nicknamed him 'Tootsie'.

Glenn also insisted that chairman, Ken Bates, invest money in the training pitches. They were rock hard in the summer and muddy quagmires in the winter, which would drain your legs of energy and inhibit practice sessions. But Glenn knew that being successful meant preparing to be successful. That is a principle anyone can take into any area of life. Our preparation needed to change and that included the surface on which we prepared for Saturday's match.

There was one new implementation in which I couldn't participate. That was when he encouraged injured players to see his faith healer, Eileen Drewery. I told him this didn't fit with the Christian faith. She was a nice person who meant well, but Eileen claimed powers for herself that weren't Christian. Glenn said he believed that Christianity was too narrow and that there were many ways to God. But I knew the Bible said differently: 'I am the way the truth and the life. No one comes to the Father except through me.' (John 14:6). These are Jesus' words, not mine. I hoped my stance on this wouldn't affect my standing with Glenn, but he was very respectful of it and didn't try and force the issue.

I found Glenn a thoroughly decent man. He gave me days off when I needed to go with Amanda and Jake to Great Ormond Street children's hospital. He spent time with me and helped me become a better midfielder. He improved my game – and not only mine. Many Chelsea players over Glenn's tenure at Stamford Bridge benefited from his coaching. Some critics say he lacked man-management skills and an ability to relate to players. That may have been true in rare cases but not overall. Suffice to say; he did care about his players a lot. And in retrospect his record with Chelsea and England was very good, which proves the point. That he lost the England manager's position for an off-the-record conversation with a reporter about his personal beliefs was a miscarriage of justice and English football lost out because of it. Glenn is one of the great footballing minds of the past fifty years and should still be coaching at the top level today.

I had arrived at a big club with a football genius as a manager. It was 1993 and the Premier League was only a year old. I replaced Andy Townsend, an excellent and very popular player for Chelsea, so I was keen to prove my worth and get off to a good start. I scored a flying header against Spurs in a preseason Makita tournament, which we won, and it was my head again with which I scored on my league debut at Stamford Bridge versus the previous year's Premier League runners-up, Blackburn Rovers – a team containing England striker, Alan

Shearer. My goal was at the famous Shed End and it began a good relationship between the Chelsea fans and me, even though we lost the game 2-1.

A few weeks later we played Manchester United at Stamford Bridge. United were the current Premier League champions and strong in every quarter. There's always a buzz when they come to town. The Bridge was packed with 40,000 fans. This was our biggest test so far under Glenn Hoddle in what had been an underwhelming first few games in terms of results. I played upfront with big Tony Cascarino that day. I had known Tony since I was fourteen and my father was his manager at Gillingham. When he was nineteen, Tony was playing for Kent non-league football club, Crockenhill, and working as a hairdresser. My Uncle Peter, who was married to my dad's sister, Valerie, was involved with Crockenhill and knew Tony. He told my dad, 'You need to get down here and see this kid. He's got potential.'

Tony was raw, but he was big, 6' 2", strong in the air and had great running power. He was unusual for a big striker in that, unlike many of his size, he could run in the channels and put good crosses in from wide positions, as well as being a massive danger himself in the penalty box. It didn't take my dad long to sign him up and, as a good will gesture, Gillingham gave Crockenhill a set of team tracksuits. So Tony Cascarino was famously signed for the sum of twelve track suits and went on to become a Gillingham favourite. Tony ably served Millwall, Aston Villa and Celtic as well as Eire – notably in the 1990 World Cup in Italy. Unfortunately, Big Cas had been a victim of some injury problems at Chelsea and struggled to win over the fans. But a hat trick in the preseason Makita tournament victory had paved the way for a good start under Hoddle. I loved playing with Cas, and for a few games we had a nice little partnership and scored a few goals. He nicknamed us 'Smash and Grab'.

We took that good form into the Manchester United match and immediately caused defenders, Steve Bruce (another of my father's former players) and Gary Pallister, a few problems. Midway through the first half Hoddle drifted out of the back three and picked up the ball in midfield. This was where he was so dangerous. He was like a top golfer who used the right club for every shot each time. This time it was as if Glenn took out a seven iron and clipped a ball into the United penalty box. Bruce cleared but only as far as the incoming Steve Clarke who has made his way forward from that right side, wing-back position. Clarke struck it well, and I saw that goalkeeper Peter Schmeichel might not be able to hold onto the ball. For hours after training at Newcastle Ossie Ardiles worked with us on following up on rebounds. It was second nature to me. Schmeichel parried. I got there before Steve Bruce and lifted it over the diving Dane and into the roof of the net. And the roof came off Stamford Bridge! We held out for a 1-0 victory even though United pressed us hard. I remember going for a late meal in London afterwards with my wife. As we came out of the restaurant, the Sunday newspapers were already on the streets. I saw my name in headlines not on the back page.... But at the top of the front page! That was a big victory and a big goal for me personally.

Nevertheless, after the euphoria of that win against Manchester United we struggled to perform with consistency, and the difficulties we had executing Glenn's new style showed in our results. Glenn was patient with us but around Christmas time we were almost bottom of the Premier League. The turning point was Southampton away. We lost 3-1 and went bottom. In the dressing room afterwards, Glenn and his assistant Peter Shreeve were critical of our performance but encouraged us to keep playing football. But that repetitive encouragement wasn't enough, and Dennis Wise knew it. Sometimes things need to be said in the dressing room, and someone needs to offer tough words, even if it challenges the management. Dennis stood up, 'Gaffer, I'm not having that. We don't need to "keep playing football". We're too soft. We need to get on that pitch and kick a few people. Then we might be able to play some football.' Although his language was a little more colourful than I put it here, that was the drift of Dennis's speech. And he was correct. We needed to earn the right to play. We needed to start working harder and, yes, start making some tough tackles, which made sure the opposition knew we were up for a fight. We needed to have an aggressive mindset.

You don't need to be the greatest tackler or the strongest player on the field in order to be aggressive. Aggression is in the mind. It's an attitude that says, 'You will not beat me. And if you want to, I will do everything to make it as hard as possible for you.' It means doing the hard things. It means putting that extra effort in to close the opposition down when they are in possession. It means making sure you are first to the loose balls in midfield. It means digging deep inside to find that resilience that comes from knowing that if you do the basic things well and consistently, your form will improve. It comes from knowing that if you fail, you might not only lose your place in the team, the team might be relegated, and you might lose your next contract, and you and your family will suffer; it comes from realizing that your career hinges on moments like these. It means acting like a man and finding that thing called courage. Winston Churchill said, 'Courage is rightly esteemed the first of human virtues…because it guarantees all the others.'

Courage might not be the first of human virtues (that, of course, is love – and I would argue that love for something fuels courage to fight for it), but courage is necessary in the face of danger and vital for the attempt to overturn impending defeat. Recovery begins with the next game, and it begins with you, the individual. You need to stop blaming your team-mates and look at your own performance. When you improve your individual performance, you will improve the team.

We won the next three games over the New Year period with victories over Newcastle United, Swindon Town and Everton. Wise's words had indeed been wise words, and as club captain his performances epitomized the spirit of it all. Dennis was a great captain and went on to be one of the best in Chelsea's history. Over the next few weeks we literally dragged ourselves off the bottom and towards mid-table in January 1994. Mark Stein, whom Glenn signed in October, had begun to hit real goalscoring form and our league improvement coincided with a great FA Cup run – a run in which I would score in every round and which would to take us all the way to the FA Cup final for the first time in twenty-four years.

***

We had a good team spirit in that first season and a few funny characters in the dressing room. Dennis Wise was always up for a prank. I remember wearing a very nice, new pair of loafers into training one day. Wisey spotted them and when I came in from training and went to put them on after showering, I found them filled with orange juice and biscuits – ruined. You had to be a bit careful with Wisey if you tried to get him back though, because he would just keep going and the pranks would get worse.

Another big character was Tony Cascarino. He could make me laugh like no one else. He and I used to travel in together from Kent – 60 miles round the M25 to Heathrow. So Big Cas and I spent hours together in the car and talked about most things in life. Cas was a bit older than me and told vivid stories of his days with the Eire squad and the manager, Jack Charlton. He seemed to have a line about everyone. I'm not surprised he's done so well in his media career. He knows his football, is very popular amongst his fellow players and isn't afraid to give honest opinion. He has always remained the down to earth lad from Crockenhill in Kent that my dad signed when he was nineteen.

The trouble with our journey round the M25 orbital was the traffic. It was awful and could sometimes double our one-hour trip. During my first winter at Chelsea, Cas and I had been late for training a couple of times in a week. Glenn Hoddle wasn't happy, understandably so. We made our case, 'But Gaffer, the traffic is terrible and gets worse with the bad weather.' Glenn barked at us, 'I don't care about the weather. You are professional footballers and you must be at training on time. Move closer to the training ground. If not, I don't care what time you leave in the morning, make sure you are on time. And if you get stuck in traffic, turn that car around and go the other way round the M25 to get here. The road runs in a circle you know.'

The next day Cas and I set off nice and early and we flew round the M25 with no hold ups at all. Training started at 10.30 am and we arrived at 9.45 am. Glenn used to get in an hour and a half before training, so we knew he would be in the building. 'I've got an idea!', said Cas, 'Follow me.' We snuck into the corridor outside the manager's room. It's laughable to think that in those days in the 1990s the only phone in the Chelsea FC manager's room at the training ground was a pay phone. Cas called it from his mobile phone. 'Hello!' I could hear Glenn's assistant, Peter Shreeve, answer from the other side of the door. 'Pete, it's Cas. Gav and I are stuck on the M25 again. Weather is terrible. Snow. We are going to be late again. Sorry Pete.' Peter told Glenn who was next to him. And Glenn exploded. 'Right, that's it. Tell 'em they're fined. They can turn around on that M25 and go the other way. I don't care what time they get here. It can be 3 o'clock this afternoon. But they will be doing a double session on their own.' Peter relayed the message back to Cas. 'Okay, Pete. Sorry, Pete. We're on our way, Pete. Gav, turn the car around!' We could hardly stifle the laughter as Cas finished the call. We gave it thirty seconds and the two of us knocked on the manager's door in front of us. Glenn opened it. 'You're right, Gaffer. It's much quicker going around the other way on the M25!!!' Glenn's face was a picture. But I think he saw the funny side…after a while.

Another dressing room comedian was John Spencer. 'Spenny' was our 5' 5" Scottish striker born in the tough Gorbals area of Glasgow. Around the training ground you would hear him before you saw him. And his wit was razor sharp. He kept the lads entertained and on their toes. One day we arrived for training. I was getting changed and kept hearing screams coming from the boot room. Spenny had brought his two 100 lb Rottweilers in with him and tied them both up directly in front of where our boots hung. Unsuspecting, and one by one, the players had gone to get their boots like any normal morning and were faced with two slobbering, snarling, giant dogs!

No one was immune to Spenny's jokes. And it wasn't too long before Glenn Hoddle's turn came. We had an oxygen chamber in the treatment room at Stamford Bridge. It was state of the art and looked like a small space shuttle, with room for only one person inside. The idea was to oxygenize the blood to maximum level in order to accelerate healing in muscle and bone injuries. The trouble is you had to be in this tiny capsule for one hour and it took time, fifteen minutes or so, to compress and decompress. This meant that you couldn't get out quickly even if you needed the bathroom! Also, it had just two tiny windows on each side and your only contact with the outside world was by a microphone through which Bob Ward, our physio, would speak and check you were okay – every fifteen minutes or so – if he remembered. The oxygen chamber was good for healing injuries, but it was not good for impatient footballers who wanted to get home early. And it was definitely not good for the claustrophobic ones.

John Spencer came in the treatment room one afternoon. Bob Ward had stepped out for a break. 'Who's in the oxygen chamber?' 'It's the boss', I said. The look on Spenny's face told its own story. 'Spenny, no! The gaffer is a bit claustrophobic.' Spenny grabbed two big towels, dived on the ground and crawled commando style across the treatment room approaching the chamber from behind, with the great Glenn Hoddle happily listening to music inside. He then threw towels over both windows and plunged Glenn into pitch blackness. Glenn began to shout and bash his arms and fists on the inside of the chamber. 'Get me out of here quick. I can't stand it. It's dark.' A few of the players had gathered around by now and were laughing hysterically. Bob Ward came rushing back into the room and we all scarpered as he ripped the towels off the windows and began to literally…decompress Glenn! When he emerged, Glenn was far from decompressed. He was furious and threatened us all with extra training unless the culprit came clean. Spenny finally owned up and was mercifully given only a sharp rebuke from Hoddle. Once more the fiery Scotsman had given us some dressing room fodder – because we all loved it when the joke was on the boss!

***

Meanwhile on the field, we began to hit it off. The FA Cup run began with Barnet FC taking us to a replay, which we won comfortably. Glenn Hoddle's brother, Carl, played for Barnet that day. He was a lovely lad and a decent footballer, who tragically died of a brain aneurism in 2008. Our route to Wembley was kind to us in terms of the teams we played and the ones we avoided. But you can only beat what is in front of you. I was scoring from midfield in the league and also managed to score in every round of the FA Cup all the way to the final. A quarter final winner against Wolves (1-0) and then a semifinal brace against Luton Town at Wembley Stadium (2-0) sent us into the final in May of 1994 against, of all teams, Manchester United.

For me personally, that season had been one of scoring winning goals, and Manchester United featured prominently. After the 1-0 home victory in September we travelled to Old Trafford in March. The Theatre of Dreams, they called it. The place is intimidating to say the least. With a 75,000 capacity, the crowd literally roars against the opposition. I received a telegram before the game from a Christian friend who was also a United supporter. It read, 'Welcome to the Theatre of Dreams, or should I say, The Den of Lions.' Hoddle set the game plan out. We would be defensively tight and hit them on the break. 'You might get one chance in the game and you have to score', he said, as we walked out.

We kept things tight and were let off a few times against a barrage of United pressure. But, just as Hoddle predicted, the chance did come. Midway through the second half: a long perfectly flighted ball from the right side of midfield from Craig Burley reached the head of Mark Stein. As the ball left Burley's foot, I started my run. I could see the gap in their defence appearing. I would make ten to twenty of these runs per game, sometimes in order to get only one chance. Stein nodded it down and now it was a race between goalkeeper Peter Schmeichel and me. He came rushing towards me from his goal-line looking like a big grizzly bear out of the corner of my eye. I knew it would be painful. Our bodies clashed at the same time, but I managed to lift the ball over his body as his studs ripped down my thigh. I spun up in the air but watched the ball bounce over the line and into the net before I hit the ground. And we held out for a 1-0 victory. Not many teams beat Manchester United home and away in the same season, and to get the winner in both was thrilling.

Even though we beat them twice in the league, we lost the FA Cup final that year. But Chelsea was on the rise and back on the map. The 'King's Road Revolution' had begun. People were talking about us more and more, and Hoddle had the fans believing again. Two weeks before the cup final Glenn Hoddle called me into his office. 'Terry Venables wants you to join the England squad for training tomorrow.' The man who signed me as a schoolboy for QPR ten years before was now the national team manager, and I had caught his eye. He was having some practice matches at Bisham Abbey, the training headquarters of the England team.

Just being around the England squad meant being on a different level. The press attention is huge, and that is just for a training session. I was nervous. I knew most of the players but still felt like an outsider and only had minutes to settle and show what I could do. I was thrown into a practice match with Tony Adams (Arsenal), Alan Shearer (Blackburn), Paul Gascoigne (Lazio) and Peter Beardsley (Newcastle). I did quite well though. Ted Buxton, who had been my father's chief scout at Gillingham FC, was now Venables's chief scout for England. He informed me a few days later that Venables wanted to play me in an England B international match the following week, but that Hoddle said it was too close to the upcoming FA Cup final and there was too much of a risk for me getting injured. I understand his reasoning, but always wonder what might have been if I had been able to play in that match. I made a couple of those England training squads in my Chelsea days.

At my best I was close to a full call up. But being close was not quite good enough.

**

Meanwhile Amanda and I had rented a house in the quaint village of Bexley in Kent. We loved being parents and also being closer to our extended family. But that year still proved quite testing. In the early part of the football season we had to make a visit to Great Ormond Street Children's Hospital in London for a specialist to see Jake and make a plan going forward. I'll always remember walking into the reception with Amanda and seeing two young parents with seven-year-old twins in wheelchairs – both with cerebral palsy. It was heartbreaking. Parenting is a hard job for anyone. But many are given children with extra challenges. This changes the shape of their parenting to some degree. Those parents need an extra dose of patience and compassion and wisdom. They also feel their child's pain when the nasty comments come or when what is normal for most kids becomes an obstacle for theirs. There was pain and parenting tears to come for us in respect to our son that we couldn't have imagined then, and that no one but Amanda and I know about. As I looked around the hospital that day it struck me how many children were suffering with various conditions and illnesses and how constant physical and emotional pain is the norm for so many families. And that was just in one city in one part of the world.

Jake was given a prosthetic, which looked like a small doll's arm with an elasticated sock on the end. We would insert his forearm into the open end of the prosthetic and the combination of natural suction and elastic sock would keep it in place. After Great Ormond Street we regularly visited the Gillingham Disablement Centre in Kent where they monitored Jake's growth and gave him new cosmetic arms as he grew bigger. This helped him develop balance as he learned to crawl. It also filled out his clothes. They don't make one-armed shirts.

Within months of Jake's birth Amanda's father, Mick, was diagnosed with leukemia, and my maternal grandmother died. My grandfather had died a few years earlier but at least she was able to hold her first great grandchild in her final days. She and my grandfather had done well making that move to England all those years ago. As she looked at Jake with his dark hair and eyes that matched hers, it must have been a satisfying moment during her final days. So, in those days, amidst life in the Premier League, we navigated the trials of life and death in our family.

In 1993 I also embarked on my first book. You may call it luck or coincidence, but how the book came to be is actually a story of God's remarkable wisdom and providence through relationships. As theologian, A. W. Tozer, once said:

> To the child of God, there is no such thing as accident. He travels an appointed way. The path he treads was chosen for him when as yet he was not, when as yet he had existence only in the mind of God. Accidents may indeed appear to befall him and misfortune stalk his way; but these evils will be so in appearance only and will seem evils only because we cannot read the secret script of God's hidden providence and so cannot discover the ends at which He aims.

Here is the story of how the book was born. When I was playing for Newcastle, I had come across Alan Comfort. Alan was a player for Middlesbrough, but he'd also been with me at QPR when I signed on as a professional player in 1984. Alan moved quickly from QPR that same year and played for Cambridge United and Leyton Orient before moving up to a big team in Middlesbrough. At Cambridge United, however, he was a team-mate of Graham Daniels (now General Director of Christians in Sport). Graham's Christian witness was so compelling that he led Alan to Jesus Christ. When Alan and I were team-mates at QPR neither of us was a Christian, but when our paths crossed again in the North East, we were both believers in Jesus as our Lord and Saviour.

However, Alan had just experienced a career-ending injury and was studying for the Anglican ministry as a vocation. Being a pastor, vicar or minister wasn't even on my radar at that time. My football career was on the up and his was ending and his path was changing. But seeing Alan battle with the disappointment of losing the game he loved, whilst maintaining his view that God is good and would provide, was exemplary. Alan was married to Jill, and still is, and they introduced Amanda and me to their friends, Dave and Heather Male. Dave was a vicar in the Anglican Church. We became firm friends with the Males and remained so after the Comforts left the North to head South for Alan's first ministry position. Dave had a friend called James Catford, who worked for publishing company, Hodder and Stoughton. He had the idea of doing a book about Alan and me – our football and faith, and the way we started together at QPR and came back together in the North of England as Christians with a completely different worldview on life and sport than when we began as kids in West London.

So, here's the timeline – stay with it! Gavin and Alan are team-mates in 1984 in West London. Alan meets Graham Daniels at Cambridge United later in 1984 and becomes a Christian. Gavin becomes a Christian a year or so later and meets Graham shortly after that. Alan and Gavin go on their football travels and end up living only minutes from each other and playing for rival teams in the North East of the country in 1990. Alan's football career is cut short. Gavin's career is accelerating. Alan introduces Gavin to Dave. Dave introduces Gavin and Alan to his friend, James. Alan goes into ministry. Gavin gets a move to Chelsea. And after multiple God-appointed friendships and connections, ten years after first meeting, in 1994 Alan and Gavin do a book together called, *Never Walk Alone*.

Certainly, the Christian has that great assurance which the book title suggests. Jesus says: 'And behold, I am with you always, to the end of the age.' (Matt. 28:20). And isn't that what everyone needs? To know God is with them in the moments of success and glory but also in the moments of dark suffering. Alan and I could both speak to that truth in our lives up to that date. Our book was published in 1994 towards the end of my first season at Chelsea. It's out of print now but sometimes I will get a message from someone saying, in some cases, how much it affected them as a young man or woman and encouraged their faith or, in other cases, how it moved them to look at who Jesus really is and at least investigate the Christian faith.

That season at Chelsea had gone very well personally – better than I ever imagined. I finished equal top scorer with Mark Stein as I bagged a good return of fourteen goals from midfield. We lost to Manchester United in the FA cup final. That was disappointing, but it wasn't devastating. The past year had taught me much about success, suffering and the sovereignty of God. It's about perspective and dealing with the highs and lows in the knowledge that God is in control and God is also good and has done something to finally deal with all suffering for those who trust in Him. There is more glory in knowing God than winning a cup final or having perfect health or immense wealth.

It was around this time that I also started a London Christian Footballers' Bible study at our house once a month. Graham Daniels and Stuart Weir from Christians in Sport would make the journey to Bexley in Kent along with half a dozen other players, and, if they were married, their wives. They were good

Sundays in the South East when Graham would give a message from the Bible, we would pray and we would sing together.

People often ask, 'Is it difficult being a Christian and a professional footballer?' I always answer that it is difficult being a Christian in any walk of life but professional football comes with some unique challenges: living out your faith under such intense public scrutiny, the massive highs and the massive lows within a few days of each other and the transitory nature of the job are three things that come to mind instantly. Southend United's Chris Powell, Charlton's Carl Leaburn and Michael Bennett, Brighton's Junior MacDougald, and two young lads I brought with me from Chelsea, Russell Kelly and Jimmy Aggrey, were included in the mix of that London footballers' meeting. The local church is always the primary place for a Christian to grow but that Bible study at my house for a few years was a good opportunity to strengthen and encourage footballers in their faith and for those players to be amongst others who were going through similar challenges in their lives.

***

Chelsea was more of a cup team than a league team in those days. The 1994/95 season – the one following the cup final – continued to prove that. Our league form was average. But we had qualified for the European Cup Winners Cup and went all the way to the semifinal. It was a remarkable achievement considering most of us had never played at that kind of level before. However, Glenn Hoddle taught us how to approach European games with a slower and more patient style – to be tactical like in a chess match, rather than the direct frantic Premier League pace to which we were accustomed. In those days you were required to play a minimum of seven English-born players in each game, which severely stretched your squad.

But Glenn bought and sold in the transfer market to give us that flexibility. Tony Cascarino left for Marseilles in the south of France, where he enjoyed a real revival of form and we signed Paul Furlong for a club record £2.3 million. Scott Minto followed from Charlton Athletic, and he became my new travel partner, roommate and good friend. Paul was a lovely man. He was extremely strong and powerful, and, although he didn't have the best goalscoring record in his Chelsea days, he went on to have a very good career in the game. Scott was a skilful, intelligent player on the field, and he transferred that intelligence and skill to his off-field, post-playing career as a Sky Sports Football League and Spanish La Liga anchorman. In fact, Scott is so clever that even his dogs are bilingual. His wife, Diana, is Columbian. So, the hounds understand Spanish and English!

That was also the season I captained Chelsea most regularly. I had been vice captain to Dennis Wise in my first season and wore the armband against Norwich for the first time. Dennis got himself into a bit of trouble with the police early on in the 1994/95 season. In a Saturday night fracas with a London black-cab driver, he kicked through the glass partition inside the vehicle. He spent a few hours in jail and had a court case on his hands. So, he was fined by the club, and Hoddle took the captaincy away from him and gave it to me. I felt a little awkward receiving the honour this way. But Dennis was fine about it all.

I liked Dennis very much. He was an excellent player with a sharp edge to his tackles, and he was an inspirational captain. Dennis also had iron lungs. He could run all day. In my time at Chelsea, his match day food consisted of a full English breakfast when he woke up and tea and biscuits a couple of hours before kick-off. And on that diet, he could outrun his opposition for the rest of the afternoon! Dennis was proud of his fitness though and I was the only one at the club who could challenge him. A competitive man, during preseason training Dennis laid down the gauntlet on a 5-mile run. 'Let's have it, Gav!' We were neck and neck all the way. I let Dennis take the pace, and he tried to shake me by increasing it and then decreasing it. Heart rate up. Heart rate down. And then he would start a conversation with me and ask me questions. Who wants to talk when you need every breath in your lungs to keep going?! Dennis was trying every tactic in the book to beat me. We hit the final 100 metres and went for a sprint finish which I won by a hair. 'A dog came out the bushes back there. Put me off my stride' was Wisey's excuse. No dog was ever seen by any of the other players that day!

Dennis and I were both very different in terms of our backgrounds and personalities and we had a few feisty arguments on the pitch, but there was always a strong mutual respect between the two of us. We both made a couple of England training squads. But Dennis was the better player. He got the call up to become a senior international and made several well-earned appearances for his country.

I captained Chelsea on several occasions throughout our European Cup run. European nights at the Bridge were scintillating, and I think one of my proudest moments in a Chelsea shirt was leading the team out in the semifinal second leg against Real Zaragoza – a team containing Brazilian world cup winner, Cafu. We were trailing 3-0 from the first leg in Spain but produced a gritty display for our fans that night winning 3-1 with goals from Paul Furlong and Mark Stein. Sadly, it wasn't enough, but we had performed admirably in our first European venture under Hoddle.

In our team on that European evening at the end of the 1994/95 season was David Rocastle. The ex-England, Arsenal and Manchester City midfielder had joined us at the beginning of the season. Rocky, as he was affectionately known in the game, had been one of the best players of our generation – a strong, fast and skilful player who could also tackle and head a ball well. And I don't think I ever met a braver player than him. When he joined us at Chelsea, he was carrying a really bad chronic knee injury. I mean his knee was misshapen it had so much scar tissue in there. He would literally hobble in warm-ups in training and needed regular pain killers as he got the knee going each day. But he never missed a session because he wanted to play so badly. We used to change next to each other at the training ground, and he had a kind word to say about everyone, as if he always tried to see the best in people. Maybe his suffering gave him more empathy for others. One thing is true though, I don't know anyone who ever spoke ill of David. And the whole football world mourned when he died of Non-Hodgkin's lymphoma in 2001 at the age of thirty-three.

He gave his all for every club he represented, but Arsenal was his first love and the team for whom he played and achieved the heights of success. Rocky's famous saying lives on in the hearts of many Arsenal fans to whom he gave so much pleasure for so many years: 'Remember, who you are, what you are and whom you represent.' There are some people in life who cross your path too briefly. David 'Rocky' Rocastle was one.

**

When I heard we had signed Mark Hughes and Ruud Gullit in the summer before the 1995/96 season, I knew we were rising to another level. Hughes, famously nicknamed 'Sparky', was a magnificent striker for Manchester United, Barcelona and Wales. Hughes was immensely strong and had legs like tree trunks. He was also very aggressive. The nicest man off the pitch, we used to say of him, 'He'd kick his own granny on the pitch.' I used to sit next to Sparky on the team bus going to away matches and really enjoyed talking to him about football and life. But I would never have guessed he would end up having a successful career as a manager. He obviously had that combination of velvet and steel that good managers have.

The dreadlocked Dutchman, Ruud Gullit, was a former captain of the Holland national team, Italian giants AC Milan, and was a Euro 1988 and Ballon d'Or winner. When you talk about being world class, Ruud was it. World Footballer of the Year. He was quite simply a footballing maestro. He stood 6' 3" tall, could run like a gazelle and had so much power in his leap that it seemed he might be able to jump over small buildings! When he was on the field, he could hold off two players at a time and appeared as if he was an adult playing football with children in the playground. He could pass, tackle and head with aplomb. He even spoke seven languages. And he made everything look effortless. After watching one Chelsea match my father said to me, 'You and Ruud both gave the ball away too much today. It's just that he did it with so much more style than you!' Thanks dad!

Ruud not only added some style on the field, he also introduced us to style off the field. In those days we would wear our iconic '90s shell suits or denim jeans into the training ground for our daily practice. As a few of us were leaving to go home one day and passing by the treatment room, there lay the great Dutchman – a fine specimen of an athlete – having his post workout massage. With arms folded behind his head as he looked us up and down, he said, in his distinctive Dutch accent, 'It has occurred to me that 75 per cent of English men cannot dress properly!' We started laughing. And then defender, Frank Sinclair, piped up, 'Well, I'm the other 15 per cent !!!' Frank was better at football than maths!

However, continental players like Gullit did bring an all-round awareness to the dressing room. How you presented yourself was important. Of course, clothes aren't everything by any means. But cleanliness and smartness of appearance is also connected to attitude of mind. Today, it often seems it is a case of dress in whatever makes you feel comfortable. Comfort, not appropriateness, is the driving force. Little things make a difference. I advise young men to dress smartly within their means in a way that shows they are ready for work. It's easy to be scruffy. It takes effort to be smart. And it shows an awareness of propriety and concern for others. Our dressing room attire livened up significantly after Ruud appeared on the scene – another one of the fruits that Glenn Hoddle's 'King's Road Revolution' had borne.

Gullit and Hughes also smashed the wage structure at Chelsea. They were reportedly earning £1m a year, which far outweighed the best paid players at the club to that date. Before that time, I remember Dennis Wise and I fighting with Chairman, Ken Bates for an extra £50 on our team win bonus. There were players in the first team on £75- 100,000 per year. But the addition of Gullit and Hughes to the pay scale didn't produce jealousy as far as I know because they were world-class players. Nevertheless, it did set a precedent and made coming to Chelsea a more attractive option for other top players. The addition of Romanian international wing back, Dan Petrescu, added yet another dimension to our team. He could really play and had a very sharp football mind. He would ghost forward from defence into dangerous attacking positions and was able to both create and score goals.

It takes time to build a new culture in an organization, but Hoddle was gradually growing something good at Stamford Bridge. In February 1996 we beat Middlesbrough 5-0 at home and produced perhaps our most complete performance to that date. I scored three goals that day – the first hat trick scored for Chelsea in the Premier League, and I remain to date one of only three Englishmen ever to score a Chelsea hat trick in the Premier League. The other two are Frank Lampard and Tammy Abraham. The wing back system and Gullit playing in midfield that day worked like a well-oiled machine and gave fans a glimpse of the future at Chelsea. Later that season we reached the semifinals of the FA Cup against Manchester United but lost 2-1 at Villa Park with a young David Beckham scoring the winner for the Reds. A few weeks later Glenn Hoddle left the club to accept the England Manager's job. It was a shock for the fans, and I was personally disappointed. But when your country calls it's hard to resist and Glenn was keen to coach England's best players and pitch his tactical mind against the world's best managers.

After Hoddle accepted the England post, Chelsea chairman, Ken Bates, acted swiftly and appointed Ruud Gullit as player manager. In the close season Ruud paid a club record fee of £4 million for Italian international Roberto Di Matteo. He then added an Italian football legend in Gianluca Vialli. During preseason and in keeping with our Italian theme we travelled to Genoa to play Sampdoria in a friendly match. Both Gullit and Vialli had played for Sampdoria in the past and were treated like gods when we arrived in Italy. During the match the ball popped loose in midfield, and I went into the tackle with Sampdoria midfield general, Roberto Mancini. I had always admired Mancini as a player but on this occasion he lifted his foot over the top of the ball and ran his studs straight down my shin from the knee to the ankle. He could have broken my leg. A professional knows when another has tried to intentionally injure them. This was not an accident. It was calculated and completely out of order.

I rarely lost my temper on the football field. But this time I did. As I was writhing on the ground in pain I kicked out at Mancini as he walked by. Within seconds I was surrounded by five Sampdoria players. The referee's view was blocked, and I received a few kicks and punches to the body and head before our players dived in to help me out. I managed to complete the match, but the leg was painful and swollen. That night we went out to a restaurant – the red carpet was rolled out for Gullit and Vialli and we were given free food and drink. Then in walked Mancini – a big friend of Vialli – looking like something out of Italian GQ. To be fair to him, he came over to me and apologized without qualification. But as he walked away, he turned around and winked at me. The look in his eye said it all, 'You shouldn't have messed with the Sampdoria Mafia!'

There was a buzz around the club now with the star signings and our superstar manager. We even had former Dutch superstar Marco van Basten join us for training one day. Maybe a little of the 1960s King's Road swagger was returning. Sadly though, the appointment of Gullit as manager was the beginning of the end of my Chelsea career. Great players do not always make great managers, and this was unfortunately the case for Ruud Gullit. Unlike Kevin Keegan he lacked man management technique. And I found myself a recipient of his poor handling of players. After the arrival of Di Matteo, I could see that I wasn't going to be a starter for Ruud. But the problem was he never once pulled me aside and explained this. He never told me his thoughts and that maybe I was going to be a squad player in his tenure. Instead I would go in on a match day and my name might or might not be written on the team board. It was the same for everyone. You could be in the team one match and not even on the bench the next. And you only found out when you looked at the team board on match day.

I was in the last year of my contract at Chelsea which meant I would be a free agent at the end of the season and could leave on a free transfer. So, I called a meeting with Gullit to discuss my future. He refused to see me on his own but insisted that backroom staff, Gwyn Williams and Graham Rix, were present. 'Ruud, it seems from the way things have panned out over preseason that I am not in your plans as a first team starter. I understand you've brought in some big-name players, and I'm willing to fight for my place. I want to stay here but with my contract coming to an end in a few months, if I'm not in your plans, maybe I should leave now and at least the club will get a fee for me.'

Ruud didn't say too much but seemed okay about the meeting – as if he would consider what I said at least. But after that he never spoke to me again, and I was sent to train with the reserves. It was the lowest time of my career to that date, and I knew it was only a matter of time before I left. I had captained Chelsea Football Club 44 times and played 134 times scoring 27 goals in three full seasons and yet Ruud afforded me little respect. I was not the only one. He did the same with John Spencer and David Rocastle. Dennis Wise actually went to Ruud's house to tell him he needed to communicate with the players and treat them a little better. Maybe he took heed to some extent in the following year when, after I had left, he won the FA Cup against Middlesbrough and brought home Chelsea's first silverware for twenty-six years. But it wasn't long before he fell out with Ken Bates over money, and Bates dismissed him saying that he never cared for Gullit's 'arrogance'.

Of course, pride is a problem for all of us to some degree. The pride of man is the cause of so much relational and economic strife: it is our downfall so many times. Look around the world today and see the root cause of poverty, rape, racism, genocides, wars and so on. It is because of the seed of pride in man. We say, 'Pride goes before a fall.' But that saying originates in the Bible which says, 'Pride goes before destruction, and a haughty spirit before a fall' (Prov. 16:18). This is the case for all of us. It is this pride that closes our ears to listening and learning and it ruins character.

Ruud's man management failure followed him to Newcastle where he refused to give crowd favourite, Rob Lee, a shirt number after taking away his number 7 jersey that he had worn with such passion for many years. He also famously fell out with England captain and Newcastle's best player, Alan Shearer. It climaxed when he left him on the bench for a match against archrivals, Sunderland, at home. That was the final nail in Gullit's coffin on Tyneside. Shearer was simply too talented and held too much sway with the fans for Gullit to survive.

Ruud did buy Gianfranco Zola for Chelsea though. And I was privileged to know him briefly before I left the club. Zola's first day of training was memorable. There was a buzz around the dressing room because everyone knew we'd signed one of the world's best players. Zola had been Diego Maradona's understudy at Napoli at the beginning of his career and went on to become a top national team player. He was small – five foot five – but incredibly skilful and like Lionel Messi today could do things other players couldn't even imagine. He was also an expert at free kicks. Before Beckham became 'the free kick man', Zola already was.

We had a practice game on his first morning at the club. Zola was on the opposite team to me. Early on the ball was zipped into his feet and he started to make a run down the line in a wide position. I thought I'd welcome him to London and Chelsea. So, I steamed over and slid in for a tackle. In one moment, he moved the ball from his right foot to his left and went past me as if I wasn't there. I was left sliding off the pitch. A few minutes later, a free kick was given for Zola's team – maybe twenty-five yards from goal. Gullit pointed to Gianfranco so he stepped up. Kevin Hitchcock was in goal and had lined up his wall. Zola took three steps back and then whipped the ball over the wall and into the top corner. All the lads were still applauding when he put the ball down again. Hitchcock knew where Zola was going to place the ball, but he was helpless to stop it as Gianfranco scored again and then he did it again. It was a remarkable performance on his first day under pressure like that.

But here's the thing. After we finished our session and were about to hit the showers, Gianfranco took a bag of balls, set up some yellow training mannequins, made a wall with them twenty yards from goal and practised on his own on a side pitch for half an hour. Gianfranco Zola was an unassuming man despite all his success. And he proved it in that he never took his skills for granted even at his stage and level. It's hard to get to the top. It's even harder to stay there. Players are not born great. They become great. There are many qualities that great players have. One is their appetite to work harder and longer than the next man and to refuse anything less than precision and perfection. Gianfranco Zola was a truly excellent player, and it is no wonder he was considered by the fans to be Chelsea's greatest ever player in 2003. His ability and humility on the field literally won the affections of fans from around the globe.

***

Every reader knows the bittersweet nature of life. No one's world is without moments of pain and moments of pleasure. And it is perhaps never more deeply felt than in occasions of life and death. My final few months at Chelsea were marked by both. I awoke on the morning of October 23rd 1996 to the news that the Chelsea Vice Chairman, Matthew Harding, had tragically died the night before in a helicopter crash as he was returning from our away match at Bolton Wanderers. I was not in the squad that travelled to the match, so I only found out the next day when a call from the club came to break the sad news. Matthew was a lifelong Chelsea fanatic who became one of Britain's top 100 richest men and who invested £26.5 million into the club in 1993. We all liked him. He was genial, down-to-earth, and basically just a fan who lived the dream at his beloved club. So, his unexpected death was felt by fans and players alike. It is fitting that the North Stand of Stamford Bridge was renamed the 'Matthew Harding Stand' in his honour.

Moments like these often make us pause for thought and gain perspective. Things that seemed to matter aren't as important anymore. What is the big deal if I am not in the first team at Chelsea and the manager is not treating me well? Life is fragile. Life is short. One thing is for certain we will all die. Then what? Is there life after death? Heaven or hell? The Bible tells us yes there is and understanding the end of all things dictates the decisions you make in the present. There is a verse written by the Apostle Paul, which says, 'For me to live is Christ and to die is gain.' In other words, whilst he lives on earth he lives by faith for the honour of Jesus and in obedience to Him. But if he dies, he gets to be with Jesus in heaven. So, death is gain. Its win-win for the Christian and death holds no fear for him or her. I got to know a few Christian football fans over the years. One family contacted me at Chelsea. A relative had died and they wanted the ashes scattered on the Stamford Bridge pitch. They asked me to do it and to pray for them. As we stood in the centre circle on a cold midweek winter's afternoon, it was a great thing to see that even in their grief they had the hope and joy of knowing their relative was in heaven and they would see him again one day.

But if 1996 was marked by a sad death at Chelsea it was also a year of life for my family.

***

In the summer of 1996 family life was in full bloom for the Peacocks and our number increased again. On June 3rd we were blessed by the birth of our second child, Ava. Although the issue with Jake's arm wasn't genetically caused, we were told that we were still statistically more likely to have another child with the same condition. Amanda had several scans during this pregnancy, but it wasn't until I held my little girl in my arms and counted ten fingers and toes that I believed it to be true. Ava's birth was much less traumatic than Jake's. Mercifully Ava came after only four hours of labour for my wife compared to two gruelling days with Jake. Ava loves to remind Jake that he has always caused more problems for us than she did! During her pregnancies it was an amazing thing to see the strength and courage of my wife, Amanda, and the miracle of new life, which she had received, nurtured and grown inside her body for nine months. Never were our differences more obvious. Throughout each term I watched as her belly grew and began to move from the inside out with an alien-like leg or arm looking like it was trying to break out. I used to ask her, 'Doesn't that feel weird?' and she would answer, 'It feels the most natural thing in the world!' All the time I was thinking, I'm so glad I don't have to do this! However, the obvious thing is, I was not made to do this.

Men and women have different strengths. It surprises many people to know that the average man has 1000 per cent more testosterone flowing through his body than the average woman. On average men can lift more weight, run faster and are more powerful in sports. So, for example, the fastest male 100 metres sprinter is way faster than the fastest woman. But women are strong in different ways. They live longer on average. And they give birth. Men go down for two weeks with the 'man flu'. If it were up to us the human race would cease to exist! Women are made with the capacity to give life. Of course, there are some circumstances which prevent this. But only a woman can give birth. Now with our beautiful Ava Eleanor Peacock in our lives, our little team was complete and although life at work was not the most pleasant at that time, home was a place of life and love.

At the beginning of the 1996/97 season at Chelsea, Gullit continued to shun me and after a few games in the reserve team my old Newcastle United team-mate Mark McGhee, who was now manager at Wolves, showed interest in buying me. Wolves was a big club but, more interesting than Wolves, was an offer from Strasbourg in France. They wanted a playmaker and I seriously considered moving to the French-German border and being their number 10. Tony Cascarino's success in France had sparked my interest in the French Ligue 1 and the continental way of life and football. I spoke with the agent trying to broker the deal. I was only just twenty-nine and in top condition, and at one point in the conversation Amanda and I actually thought we might be packing our bags again and moving to mainland Europe.

But then my old club Queens Park Rangers came calling, and it didn't take me long to decide to come 'home'. I wouldn't experience the great days of Chelsea cup wins and league championships or the big money that would come with the arrival of the Russian billionaire chairman, Roman Abramovich. But I loved Chelsea Football Club and was proud to wear the blue shirt in the era I played. As sometimes happens in football you are here today and gone tomorrow in the middle of a season and don't get the chance to say goodbye to fans, staff or team-mates. In the November of 1996, after three and a half years and some wonderful days at Stamford Bridge, I left quietly but with head held high – pleased to have been part of the 'King's Road Revolution'.

8

COMING HOME:
BACK TO LOFTUS ROAD

In the spring of 1996, Queens Park Rangers had been relegated from the Premier League, so the club still had a squad with some excellent players like Trevor Sinclair, Mark Hately, Simon Barker, Andy Impey and Alan Macdonald. Former Arsenal coach Stuart Houston and his assistant, Bruce Rioch, were resolved to take the club back up at first attempt. Chairman/owner Chris Wright had financial resources. He was the music industry executive who co-founded Chrysalis records which produced acts such as Blondie, Ultravox and Spandau Ballet. Wright had also been a QPR fan for twenty-five years. He put his money where his mouth was by paying over £3 million for John Spencer and me from Chelsea. It felt good to be back at Loftus Road and play at the club where I started. I walked onto the pitch after signing my new contract and memories flooded back as I looked at the terraces I'd swept as an apprentice back in the 1980s. Now at twenty-nine years old, ten years after I left, I was returning as an experienced player with over 350 league and cup appearances under my belt and hopefully a few good years left in me.

Oasis and the Spice Girls were rocking the charts. And David Beckham, at twenty-one, was rocking the football world scoring on the first day of the season from the halfway line for Manchester United against Wimbledon FC. The Premier League was getter bigger and wealthier, and so were the players. But Beckham was about to change the face of modern-day football with his relationship to Victoria 'Posh Spice' Adams of the Spice Girls. Over the next fifteen years David Beckham would become more than a player, helped by Victoria and her profile. When they married, the Beckham name would become a brand and David led the way in the growing phenomenon of players who had higher off-field profiles than they did on the field. He advertised everything from Calvin Klein underwear to Hugo Boss suits to Ray-Ban sunglasses. The fashion and cosmetics lists are endless. The Beckhams were cleverly managed and didn't miss a photo opportunity. But there is no doubt David was one of the best footballers of his time. His list of silverware and personal achievements in the game speak for themselves. I'm sure he enjoys his wealth, but it came as a result of hard work and discipline beyond measure. Beckham was a role model in the way he maintained his hunger for the game and wasn't sidetracked by the media circus that constantly surrounded him. The money came because he was that good. Former Manchester United manager, Sir Alex Ferguson, said he was that good because he worked so hard 'to achieve accuracy which even other world class players would not care about'.

The Premier League was the place to be. The best players in the world wanted to play there. And having played in that league, John Spencer and I joined QPR with a return there in mind. We raised the standard around QPR immediately and I really thought we would have enough strength in the squad to make the play-offs that season. Spenny was scoring goals freely and gave a return of 17 in 25 league appearances for the rest of that season. Two games stand out for me that year: both of them are memorable for great moments. First was when we played Port Vale away for the most extraordinary comeback in which I had ever been involved. We were absolutely terrible in the first half and they were smashing us 4-0 by half time. Confidence had visibly drained from the team. We knew we were in for a roasting from Houston and Rioch at half time. Spencer sat in the corner of the dressing room with a towel over his head, looking as if somehow it would protect him from the barrage of criticism that was coming our way. But we deserved it. Yet I looked up and saw good players around me – Trevor Sinclair, Andy Impey, John Spencer – begin to stir. And we came out with a different resolve in the second half.

When you are playing badly you need to go back to basics and just start doing simple things well again. We did that and began to improve, but the game turned when our left back Rufus Brevett cleared a ball off the line – a ball that actually went over the line. However, the referee didn't view it that way and waved play on. In these days of VAR (Video Assistant Referee) the goal would have been given, we would have been five down and would certainly have lost the match. But here was a let-off and within a few minutes Port Vale scored an own goal and it was 4-1. Our talented winger, Andy Impey, then fired in a stupendous volley and midfielder Paul Murray used his pace to add to that with a delicate chip to make it 4-3. Finally, in injury time, with only a couple of minutes left, John Spencer fired into the corner with his left foot to tie the game: a game which still goes down as QPR's greatest comeback in many people's minds. Never was there a better expression of the well-known saying, 'Football is a game of two halves.'

The second memorable game contained the greatest goal I experienced in a match. We played Barnsley at home in the FA Cup in February of 1997. We went 1-0 down and then I equalized with perhaps my best goal in a Rangers shirt. After linking up with John Spencer in midfield I burst past two defenders and rifled a twenty-five-yard shot in the top corner at the beloved Loft End. However, the game was memorable not for that goal but for our third goal in the match. Spencer put in a deep cross from the right. It was one that posed no threat and as I watched the flight of the ball, I held my run because I thought it would either be cleared by their defender or held up and knocked back to me by our striker. But Trevor Sinclair had other ideas. Finding himself in a central striker position, instead of trying to knock the ball back to me or anyone else, he acrobatically sprang into the air and with his back to goal connected with the ball and produced a bicycle-kick: the purest one I've seen. It flew into the top of the net. The keeper was helpless. It was voted Goal of the Season and goes down as one of the all-time best FA Cup goals.

During this time, I also connected with the club chaplain, Dave Langdon, who became a real friend to me. Dave was an ex-British Navy man, and he was perfectly suited to be a pastor in the hustle and bustle of the volatile Shepherd's Bush. As dangerous as his ministry could be at times, Dave would say to me how much he loved The Bush and its multicultural feel. Of course, Dave knew as a Christian that Jesus died for people from every tribe and tongue – every nation in the world. And he was keen to reach people from nations right next to QPR's stadium in multi-cultural West London. I would often see Dave at the training ground on a Friday and give him a ride home. We would chat about football, life and the things of God. He'd always find me on a match day and pray for me – sometimes even in the tunnel before I went out for a warm-up. He could take the banter from the other players and they all liked him. He even ran a little Bible study with me and a young player, Matthew Brazier.

***

Back at home, Jake was thriving, active and adventurous, and Ava grew lovelier each day. She looked like a doll as her hair began to grow and ringlets began to form. But she also had the energy to keep up with Jake. We now had a boxer dog too, so life in the Peacock household was full. My sister, Lauren, had married a good man, Andrew Dodd, who worked in the financial accountancy business in London. He was an Arsenal fan and yet a faithful follower of Charlton and Chelsea after he married my sister. I had always been protective of my sister growing up and hoped for her to find a good husband. Andy is that – though I always tell him that he landed on his feet marrying my sister. He and I have always got on well – even when he nearly beat me in a running race around our garden when I was playing for Chelsea! Lauren and Andy had a little girl, Celine, who was a few months younger than Ava. Shania would follow in a couple of years and become my second niece. My parents, my sister and her husband and my mother-in-law, Mary, all lived close by. Mary was heavily involved in our lives and spent many hours with the children. A better mother-in-law a man could never have.

In addition, we spent many days with Amanda's father Mick, her step-mother Mel, and their children: Ben, Jemima and Tabitha. And her Aunt Fiona and Uncle Jim added some Scottish love whenever they visited from Dundee.

So, our children were able to know and regularly see their grandparents, uncles, aunts and cousins. We had many family days together, meals out and shared birthdays and anniversaries. Amanda and I had bought a beautiful, early twentieth-century farmhouse in Bexley Village, so between football matches we were refurbishing and extending it. It was a time of life and growth. Those were happy, sunny days.

***

That first season back at QPR ended with just missing the play-offs and then it was the close season and a six-week rest. I always used to look forward to the end of season break. Thirty, forty or fifty top-level matches plus daily training takes its toll on the body and mind, so a good amount of time for recovery is useful. In fact, it is rare that a professional footballer plays a match without carrying some kind of injury or without being in some level of pain. You stretch your body to the maximum all the time. You are always recovering from kicks, bruising, cuts, muscle pain and strains – all to be ready for the next match – and all whilst training to a high level in between. There were periods when I felt like I was living on Ibuprofen. In the last couple of years of my career I would lie on the living room floor at night, legs up against the wall, trying to ease the pain in my back. It was inescapable and relentless. Mentally you are always under pressure too: pressure to perform well; pressure from team-mates; pressure from the manager; pressure from the fans; pressure from the media. Pressure is good to a certain extent as it can promote excellence and is part of the nature of the job. I enjoyed being under pressure. But by the end of a season it was good to release that pressure on body and mind and completely rest and recharge for the next season.

This particular close season my physical exertions were not quite finished. We had a fence that ran for about 100 ft down our long driveway to the entrance gates. On the other side of the fence was a public alleyway, which was regularly used as a cut through from one part of the village to another. Aimless and mischievous youths would love to kick our fence as they walked by and break the feather-board strips between the aitch rail frame. I would often return from training to find broken pieces of wood splintered across the driveway. This was happening too much, especially because they knew a footballer lived on the property. It must have given the vandals added incentive and pleasure.

It was just a few days after the end of the season and I was relaxing in the back garden on a sunny May afternoon, when I heard banging on my fence and then the sound of panels being kicked again. *That's it*, I thought. In an instant I was off my seat, sprinting across my garden into my driveway and launching myself over the fence using one hand to give me leverage. But I forgot that the alleyway was two foot lower than the level of our driveway. I don't think the teenage perpetrators knew what had hit them as I came sailing over the fence and landed like Spiderman in front of them from twelve feet above them. The shock absorbers in my knees took a hammering as well. Then the chase was on as they turned on their heels and ran into the village. But I was at top level fitness and speed, and it wasn't long before I'd captured them and was giving them a good telling-off in front of amused passers-by. That was definitely my last run of the season…and from that day forward my fence got a rest too!

I would take three weeks complete relaxation and then after our family holiday abroad – usually Florida where we would see old friends, bask in guaranteed hot weather and visit Disneyworld – I would begin my own training sessions so that preseason training wouldn't be such a shock to the system. Ask any professional footballer and I don't think one would answer that they looked forward to preseason. It's still vivid in my memory: hot days in late June early July, the smell of cut grass, morning and afternoon sessions, the pain of sore muscles, the anticipation of the agony of running without oxygen as you push the body beyond limits.

My Newcastle United manager, Kevin Keegan, always used to say, 'If you are not in discomfort at some stage in pre-season training you will never become truly fit.' That is so true.

Without some level of pain you will not get fit and improve your fitness. You have to be able to hurt your body. The old adage, 'No pain no gain' is not an old adage for nothing. Not many enjoy pain for pain's sake but if you know that the reward of supreme fitness and strength is on the other side, you can endure it. I always make this kind of comparison to 'getting fit' in the Christian life. It is always in periods of suffering that people will say their faith strengthens most.

In trials and conflict and suffering of various kinds our first inclination is sometimes to get out of the situation. We naturally want relief. But actually, what we need is to grow in faith. God's design in the trials is to strengthen fibres of faith. Just as you must push your body to distress and muscles need to be stretched and under tension in order to grow fit, it is the same in our spiritual life. It hurts, and our inclination is to give up or slow down or lessen the load so that we get relief. But muscles only grow when put under stress and we need to stay in the tension for a while. Because in the pain is the gain. And so it is with God and trials. It is in the tension and through suffering that God strengthens the muscles of faith.

***

The close season flew by. And after joining midway through the previous campaign and just missing the play-offs, John Spencer and I were set for a full season and excited about our chances of gaining promotion back to the Premier League. Trevor Sinclair was a match-winner: powerful and skilful and capable of doing the unusual; not a great goal-scorer but a scorer of great goals as his bicycle-kick goal in the FA Cup proved. He was hot property as we went into the next season (1997/98) and it was unsettling for the squad. If we were going for promotion, we needed to keep Sinclair. But from his point of view and with top Premier League clubs interested, he needed to go.

Stuart Houston had been assistant manager at Arsenal under George Graham for many years and more recently under Bruce Rioch. When he was offered the QPR job, he brought in Bruce as his assistant, like my father had done with Paul Taylor at Gillingham. Stuart was an extremely decent and honourable man. I liked him instantly and I enjoyed playing for him. But Bruce was more of the manager type. With a different assistant it might have been easier for Houston to cut his teeth during his first time as a number one. But Bruce was too powerful when he spoke and that unintentionally undercut Stuart's authority with the players. As in all teams and organizations getting people in the right position is crucial for harmony. And it didn't fit to have Stuart and Bruce's roles reversed like that.

Bruce Rioch had also been a great player for Derby County and Scotland. He was a strict disciplinarian but wanted to play good football as well. He had a little bit of the Brian Clough style about him. But that meant that not everyone liked him. John Spencer and he didn't get along well. Spenny was fiery and needed to be handled astutely in order to get the best from him. If you stifled his flair, you crushed him as a player. Bruce and Spenny had a massive training ground argument one day that didn't bode well for the team or the management. Spenny was a key player for us. If he was happy and scoring, he gave us another dimension with goals and creativity. If he was unhappy, results would suffer. We began the season with a few decent results, but they fell away, as Spenny's goals dried up a little.

By this time, Houston had also paid a club record fee of £2.75m for Mike Sheron from Stoke City. Again, balance and harmony are the key to any successful team. Kevin Keegan was so insightful in the way he positioned the right players next to each other on the field. He would watch us in training and see who would link up well with whom. But just as Rioch wasn't the right partner for Houston so it was for Sheron with Spencer, who needed a more muscular player next to him to relieve the physical burden and allow him to play with freedom. Results suffered and Rioch and Houston were sacked by November 1997. I felt sad for them, and in particular Stuart. Some men are better as assistant managers than managers. That's okay. Behind every good number one is a good number two.

***

After the departure of Houston and Rioch, however, the directors of QPR appointed another number two in the number one position. Ray Harford had been Kenny Dalglish's assistant in Blackburn's Premiership-winning campaign and was widely regarded as an excellent coach. But he was another man who was actually best suited to the assistant role in my opinion, although in his early days in coaching he had done well as Luton Town's manager. The struggle continued. In early 1998, Trevor Sinclair was sold to West Ham; and, in part-exchange, striker, Iain Dowie, and defender, Keith Rowland, were brought in. I knew Rowland as a tidy left back from my playing days at AFC Bournemouth when he was a young professional. Dowie was big and exceptionally strong: not a great goal scorer, but wholehearted and brave. These two were good players but, because we lost Sinclair in the deal, from a QPR fan's perspective it was negative business. John Spencer soon followed Sinclair out the door as he headed to Everton, and all of a sudden the future for QPR didn't look quite so bright.

You never know what's around the corner in life. A year that had started with such hope when Spencer and I joined QPR ended in sadness and the departure of the manager. The year 1997 was also marked by national and global sadness at the sudden and tragic death of Princess Diana in a Paris car crash. The nation mourned. I remember the morning that the news broke. I was driving on the Embankment (which runs parallel to the River Thames). REM's track 'Everybody Hurts' was playing on the radio. It reminded me once more of the brevity of life and the universality of suffering. No one is immune: rich or poor, commoner, prince or princess. The song ends like this:

So hold on, hold on,
Hold on, hold on, hold on, hold on, hold on, hold on
Everybody hurts.

But the question is onto what do you hold? And is that person or thing able to hold you?

***

The new QPR manager, Ray Harford, had actually been at Charlton Athletic in his playing days in the 1960s and crossed paths with my father for a while. But he came to QPR with ideas of a defensive set-up in midfield that I felt didn't suit me. He wanted me to hold my ground and shield the back four. I knew this would in a large part stop my attacking creativity. But sometimes you have to do what you don't want to do for the sake of the team. I had enough experience to adapt to what the manager wanted, and although I don't think I was his cup of tea as a midfield player when he arrived at the club, he played me in the team regularly.

Things change quickly especially in football. Nothing surprised me more than when I woke one morning and read in the newspaper that Harford had signed Vinny Jones as player coach. 'Oh, no!' I thought. 'Vinny hates me!' Vinny was the famed hard man of Wimbledon FC and their infamous Crazy Gang team of the '80s and '90s. He wasn't a great player, but he was better than people gave him credit for. He did play over 500 games, and he did represent Wales. But the lasting impression Vinny left on the game was that of a fierce tough guy. He used to intimidate the opposition and particularly his opposite number. Whenever I played against Vinny in midfield he would kick, punch and do whatever else he could behind the referee's back to put me off my game. He wouldn't have lasted too long in today's game with all the camera angles able to pick up on his antics. I couldn't believe Vinny was going to be my team-mate and my coach. I thought that would be the end for me. I arrived at the training ground that morning and Vinny was already in the changing room. To my surprise and relief, I was greeted by, 'Gav!! Great to see you, mate! We will tear it up in midfield together.' If you were on the opposite team to Vinny you were his enemy and he did what he did to win, but if you were his team-mate, it was a different story.

Vinny was a larger than life character and he had incredible belief that there was no situation that he could not handle. It came as no surprise to many who knew him that he went on to become a Hollywood star and make many movies including *X-Men: The Last Stand*. When he joined QPR he was in the final stages of filming *Lock, Stock and Two Smoking Barrels* under director, Guy Ritchie, then Madonna's husband. He would train with us in the morning and be making the movie in the afternoon. What a life!

My old St Thomas Moore team-mate, Neil Ruddock, was next to join us on loan from Liverpool until the end of the season, as Harford tried to change our momentum with the influence of a few physical players. Dowie, Jones and Ruddock were big men with big personalities that could dominate and direct a dressing room. It went to the wire that season and we survived relegation by one point. We secured it in our penultimate match against Manchester City at Maine Road. We drew 2-2 and got that point that kept us up, but the game was won before a ball was kicked and Jones, Ruddock and Dowie played their part.

Here's the story. Manchester City was in the dogfight with us (and eventually got relegated), but they had a mercurial player in Georgian international, Georgi Kinkladze. Kinkladze played just behind the strikers and had the ability to score and make goals. He was also deadly from free kicks. He was the danger man. If you stopped Kinkladze, you neutralized Manchester City's attacking strength. Nerves were tense as the two teams lined up in the tunnel waiting for the referee to lead us onto the pitch with 30,000 fans filling the stadium. All of a sudden, I heard a big commotion behind me. Neil Ruddock had hold of Kinkladze and pinned him up against the wall of the tunnel with hands round his neck. Vinny Jones was lending a hand and, shall we say, strongly advising him about what would happen to him on the pitch when he got the ball. The Manchester City players tried to intervene but came up against the brick wall that was Iain Dowie as a few punches were thrown. As quick as the fracas began it ended and the referee ushered us out and onto the pitch. Talisman, Kinkladze, scored a free kick in the first minute but after that was hardly involved in the game for the rest of the afternoon and we got the result that sealed our survival. However, intimidation isn't the way to play nor is it the QPR way, and I didn't like the direction the club was going.

Despite staying in the Championship, Ray Harford didn't last much longer in charge at QPR. After a poor start to the next season, things came to a head when we lost 4-1 in a miserable display at Oxford United. Harford and Vinny Jones read the riot act to the team in the dressing room, but they ended up arguing amongst themselves. When Jones told us we were all coming in for training the next day as punishment, Harford turned to him and said that he wasn't coming in on his day off. It was comical and tragic all at once as we watched the dispute unfold. After the match the team bus dropped Ray Harford at an M40 service station where we had picked him up on the way to the match. Sadly, he discovered that some disgruntled fans had smashed his driver's side window. He said that as he drove home that night with rain lashing in through the broken window, he knew he'd lost the desire to manage QPR anymore. The next day he resigned.

I can't say I enjoyed playing under Ray, and I cannot say that I played my best football for him either, but I still learned from him and hope to some extent I won him over with a professional attitude, so that there was a mutual respect between us. Behind an often dour appearance, he was actually a very funny character and excellent company – aspects of the man that many people did not get to see. So, I was deeply saddened to hear of his death just a few years later in 2003 after a battle with cancer. Ray was fifty-nine years old. Despite his unsuccessful time at QPR, his legacy in football was that of being a good coach and a good man. With that I heartily concur.

***

When you spend ten years of your life at one club, you really get to know and love the staff and fans. And you realize how many of the staff are fans. I was privileged to get to know Sheila Marson, our club secretary, who was a woman of utmost integrity and skill. I dealt with her many times with my contract renewals or I just popped my head in to say 'hello' whenever I was at the main stadium. Sheila had a cool head and always had the best interests of the club and players in her mind throughout the good and bad times. Then there was Terry Springett, whose dad Ron Springett played for QPR in the '60s. Terry was a diehard R's fan and is still there on the day that I write, as Football Secretary. Finally, there was Daphne Biggs who was working in the office at Loftus Road when I signed as a fifteen-year-old schoolboy, and who was still there when I returned for my second spell. She was known and much loved by everyone and is still sadly missed over ten years after her death. For these people, being at QPR was more than a job, it was their passion.

But what about the fans? Every club has their iconic supporters. You know. The ones whom you recognize week after week as they faithfully attend the matches home and away whatever the weather. They often add flair and fun to the occasion. 'Burger Ben' was one of those people at QPR. He would wear a massive Mexican sombrero on a match day when he turned up with his sons. We called him 'Burger' Ben because his job entailed supplying London restaurants, like Planet Hollywood, with meat. Sometimes the lads were able to buy some great burgers from him! I became friends with Ben, and we are still in touch today. A kinder man you'd fail to meet. There were so many others. Like Geraldine Field who would always give me chocolates after a match and send me messages of encouragement. And there was Brian Melzack who would chat for hours about football with me on the phone. These were the kinds of people who would wait for an hour and a half after a match just to say 'Hi', 'Well played' or 'Hard luck' as you were leaving the stadium – win, lose or draw.

Football fans can be brutally funny though. One time during a match the ball went into the crowd at the away end. I came over to retrieve it but one particular fellow kept hold of it as he looked down at me from six rows up and shouted, 'Oi Peacock, you're not as good as your old man!' Then his mate next to him piped up. 'His old man? He's not as good as *my* old man…and he's eighty!' When the ball was finally given back to me, I could hardly take the thrown-in I was laughing so much.

So, a football club is about more than the football on the pitch. It's about real people who love their club and the beautiful game. Sir Bobby Robson summed up a football club with emotional eloquence in his book about his time at Newcastle United FC, *My Kind of Toon*:

> What is a club in any case? Not the buildings or the directors or the people who are paid to represent it. It's not the television contracts, get-out clauses, marketing departments or executive boxes. It's the noise, the passion, the feeling of belonging, the pride in your city. It's a small boy clambering up stadium steps for the very first time, gripping his father's hand, gawping at that hallowed stretch of turf beneath him and, without being able to do a thing about it, falling in love.

Many of you who are reading this know that it's not just the players, coaches and their families that suffer when the club doesn't do well or gets relegated or goes into financial administration; it's the staff, from the lady who does the laundry to the club secretary – and it's the fans who come home and away who suffer too. So, when things are bad, the man you appoint at the helm must be able to rally the troops and be an inspiration with all these different factors playing in. Gerry Francis was the perfect man for that job. When he took over after Harford left, the whole place was given a lift. Gerry had been QPR and England's captain in the 1970s. He had also led the club as manager to their highest Premier League finishes in the 1990s before taking over at Tottenham Hotspur and, doing so well, he was at one point in the running for the England national team manager's job.

Gerry's impact was instantaneous, and I absolutely loved playing for him. He was fair-minded and always said he liked to treat people as he would like to be treated. But you did not cross Gerry. He was scared of no man and was mentally and physically tough. And this is something he made known to the players early on. He joined in a five-a-side in the first week of his return to Loftus Road, and he took no prisoners. When Gerry tackled you, even then at his age of forty-seven, you stayed tackled. He was also a thinker. We started a little later in the morning (11 am) under Gerry because he liked to allow the rush hour traffic to die down so that players would spend less time in their cars. It could easily take an hour or so for most players to battle across London to the training ground and spending that amount of time in a car was often a cause of back issues which led to further injuries. That was shrewd decision-making.

So, Gerry was considerate. But he was also demanding. To increase our fitness he introduced a rigorous running session once a week. We called it, 'Terror Tuesday'. I still remember feeling sick with nerves driving into West London on those mornings just thinking of the pain to come. Terror Tuesday consisted of twelve runs with ninety seconds rest in between. We ran from penalty box to penalty box and back again in different configurations. Sometimes one run contained a treble configuration of runs within it. Players would be on their knees throwing up by the third run, knowing there were nine to go. There were times when my lungs felt like they would burst, and I would not be able to recover my breath. The session was a man-killer and required as much mental strength as physical fitness. Gerry's philosophy was that if you could get through the pain of Terror Tuesday then Saturday would hold no terrors for you.

Finally, Gerry was a tactician. We did hours of team play so that every player knew his job. The best coaches make systems simple for players and employ systems that suit the strength of their players. Gerry did this very well. We not only spent hours on the training ground working on team structure, we sat for hours in the video room analyzing the previous game and our performance. On a Sunday Gerry would spend time at his house editing the ninety minutes of a match down to forty minutes of highlights (or lowlights!). We would gather at the training ground on Monday morning and wait for him to come downstairs from his office with the video in his hand. If we'd won and played well, we'd be chirpy and joking with one another. If we'd lost and played badly, we would be like a room full of men awaiting execution.

Gerry would go through the good, the bad and the ugly of the game individually and corporately, and there was no escaping the all-seeing eye of the video camera. The good stuff was praised. But if you made a bad pass, it was there for all to see. If you didn't mark your man at a set piece, you couldn't deny the video evidence. Our defender, Jermaine Darlington, once tried to argue with Gerry saying that he hadn't let his opponent run past him with the ball.

'No way gaffer. I didn't let my man go!'

Gerry simply fast forwarded the video to that part of the game in question and pressed 'play'.

'There he goes straight past you, Jermaine', he said.

Then Gerry rewound the tape and replayed it, 'There he goes again, Jermaine. Did you see him? Straight past you.' Rewind! 'And there he goes again.' Rewind! 'Oh look! And again.' Jermaine knew he was a defeated man and had to concede to the truth. The rest of the team was crying with laughter. Watching those match videos might not have been the easiest thing to endure sometimes but they created a culture of conscientiousness and honesty amongst the players.

Gerry was a breath of fresh air at the club: a top manager and a powerful leader. I was a senior player in my early thirties then, but with plenty of games left in me. Gerry treated me well and would often have me in his office to chat and hear my thoughts. I respected him hugely and I always say that if he had continued at QPR after I came to the end of my playing days, I would have followed the coaching route under his tutelage. But that wasn't to be.

We stabilized in Gerry's first season in charge (1998/99). That season saw the emergence of Richard Langley through the youth system and into the first team, scoring on his first-team full debut and ensuring our first win under Gerry Francis. I took Richard under my wing. He was a QPR youth product like myself and I instantly liked his attitude. He was respectful to older professionals, but he had excellent ability and a bit of an edge to his game. Injuries prevented Richard from having a career in the Premier League, even though he became a Jamaican international player. Suddenly I was looking at young players like Richard and realizing my age. Firstly, I felt more like an older brother or father to them. Secondly, when I mentioned Duran Duran or Wham they said, 'Who?'!

Gerry also signed two strikers: Chris Kiwomya from Arsenal and Swedish international, Rob Steiner, from Bradford. With Kiwomya's speed and guile and Steiner's aerial strength and all-round ability we had enough in the team to narrowly avoid the relegation threat which faced us after a bad start under Harford. In the 1999/2000 season we looked good for the play-offs but ran out of steam at the same time as losing Steiner for too many games. That was our big chance under Gerry Francis. And we missed it.

***

Although we brought in young defender Clarke Carlisle and striker Peter Crouch for the beginning of the following season (2000/2001) we couldn't get a string of wins going. Clarke Carlisle was a swashbuckling centre half. Standing 6' 3" and powerfully built, he was a very confident young man, maybe overconfident, and he breezed into the club with an air of invincibility. He was fancied by many to go to the top of the game. One of the rituals every new player was made to endure at QPR was singing a song before the rest of the team in the hotel restaurant the night before their first away game. They had to stand on a chair after dinner and perform a number of their choice until the lads let them sit down. This was a terrifying prospect to most, and the players were not an easy crowd to please. But Clarke took the mic., as it were, and sang like a professional. As a senior player I'd seen this type of personality before, so being captain of the team I would give him a lot of verbal testing to see if he had the character to underpin his blasé exterior. But Clarke responded well. 'Skipper', he would say, 'I can beat anyone for banter but you.'

Underneath, however, I saw that he was actually quite an insecure, frightened young lad and the outward bravado was just a cover that hid a very sensitive person. He took a little while to settle at QPR but put in some good performances and was rightly recognized by England U21s. He was doing well right up to the moment he ruptured his cruciate ligament. I remember it like yesterday. The ball was played back to him near the halfway line in one of our evening matches at Loftus Road. As he lunged in for the tackle and made contact with the opposition player, I heard him scream and saw him twist. Professional footballers develop instincts about these things, and I knew it was bad. The poor lad was going to be out for a long time and might not even make it back at all. It was the kind of injury we all dread. I called him on the phone to cheer him up a few days later. But what I didn't realize was that Clarke also had an alcohol and gambling problem and had suffered from depression for a while.

He didn't reveal it to me in that phone call, but it all came out a few months later. It just goes to show that you can train and play with someone week in and week out and not know about mental health issues that lead to different vices. It is one of my big regrets that I didn't press in deeper with Clarke, especially in those dark days after his injury. When it broke publicly about his troubles, I knew there was a level of responsibility that Clarke must take for his own actions, but looking back I feel I let him down as his captain. I think perhaps I could and should have helped him more.

Depression has plagued Clarke through his life after football and, after several suicide attempts, he has spoken publicly about the need to ask for help. Depression is a major issue in the world. Many people are wired that way, or an event happens which sends them into a tailspin out of which it appears there is no way out. It's a terrible thing and the worst symptom is a sense of hopelessness. I counsel people who are suffering this way to read the book of Psalms in the Bible. Here you find prayers, laments and praises that cover every human emotion. It's as if the psalms provide an X-ray of your soul. But they point you to the one true source of hope and the remedy for pain. A merciful, loving God.

Back on the field and another relegation battle was on our hands. Peter Crouch ('Crouchy' was the inventive nickname we gave him!) was proving a great player. At 6' 6", and very lean, he did not look like a typical footballer – more like a basketball player – and so Crouchy was inevitably the target for many jokes. On his first-team debut, some of the players wheeled in the life-size plastic skeleton from the physiotherapist's room, left it by Crouchy's changing spot and put his match shirt on it. He also took immense stick from the fans – our own as well as the opposition. Some of it was good-humoured, but a lot was brutal. Nevertheless, Peter Crouch had character. He was made of the good stuff and he rose above it and battled on. He also had immense talent. His touch on the ball was like velvet. His flicks and passes were executed like brush strokes from a great artist. His skill and vision were at another level to any striker in the league. It is no wonder that he went on from QPR to have a career at the very top, playing for Aston Villa, Liverpool,

185

Tottenham Hotspur and Stoke – even becoming an England international, amassing forty-two caps and scoring twenty-two goals.

Clarke Carlisle came back from his injury and played a good number of games in his career. But even as Crouch's career went up and on, Clarke must wonder if it hadn't been for one lunge, one tackle and one moment in a game, he too might have hit the heights like Peter. That's the way it is in football. Moments decide games and careers. Injuries play their part.

***

The treatment room at a football club is a humbling place to be. I didn't suffer from major injuries. But I found myself there several times over in my career, particularly towards the end of my playing days. While you're on the physio's table you might be the team's star player, but you have as much influence on a Saturday as the ticket sellers and the tea lady. The treatment room is also a place where insecurities are revealed. Footballers know they have a short career and a limited length of contract. Alongside this they know that injury can cut that career short or severely impact it. Injury takes you out, another player takes your place and then that player keeps you out. It takes mental strength to deal with an injury and work your way back to match fitness. Hence players with long-term damage sometimes get extremely down or even depressed. Consequently, part of the physio's job has always been to get the player physically fit and keep him mentally strong. That's a tough mandate. The treatment room levels players, and it also reveals where someone's identity lies.

In all of us there is a desire for identity, a desire to belong and be accepted, and a desire for glory. Footballers find this in simply being a footballer. They find pleasure in the sense of belonging and camaraderie. And their desire for glory is fulfilled in victory on the field, excellence of performance and adulation from the fans. However, if your identity is found in being a 'footballer' – or being in any other sport or job – when doubt is cast on the stability of that identity, your world is rocked.

Think about your life. I'm sure many can say, if a certain bad thing hadn't happened things could have been much more prosperous for them. Maybe you even look at others and envy the good fortune they have had and assume the relative ease with which they got it. You look at your life and you are unfulfilled and feel you missed out. If your identity and sense of purpose and satisfaction is tied up in material success, perfect health and a trouble-free life, then you will soon be disappointed. Football is a great game. In my opinion, it's the best. But if you look to football or anything else for ultimate identity, it won't last, it won't satisfy, and it won't eventually save you. Only in knowing who God is and who we are in relation to Him do we find our identity – one that lasts. Only God can save us from embracing false identities and give us ultimate purpose and satisfaction. To this we will turn later.

***

Clarke Carlisle was out for the season, our league form was poor, and then we got thumped 6-0 by Arsenal in the fourth round of the FA Cup in late January 2001. Add to this the rumblings of financial difficulties behind the scenes and it did not surprise me when Gerry Francis decided to step away from the job and let former QPR player, Ian Holloway, step in as manager at the end of February. Gerry knew the ship was leaking and he was struggling to stop it without money to invest. A month before he left the helm, we called a players meeting. A few of the lads were moaning about Gerry's tactics, the videos, the running sessions and so on. It's funny how easily we can find fault with the very things that have been instrumental in past success. We become quick to blame others for our own failures.

I stood up and addressed the players saying that we needed to take responsibility for our own performances. We had all been underperforming, myself included. I said we needed to own that, to trust Gerry, and to pull together because if we were relegated, we would all suffer – our families above all. The players listened – maybe not all agreed but some did. However, something in me stirred that day: a desire to lead a group like that. Maybe management was going to be for me after all. In addition, I'd begun to see the bigger picture better as a senior man and to care about other players in a deeper way as by then I had a lot of experience of the trials of football: injuries, bad form, defeat and more. I was looking out for one or two younger players like Langley. I felt a need to pass on the baton.

I also saw the difficulties of being a foreign player trying to settle in a new country. For instance, Anti Heinola, our Finnish defender, always looked miserable. We used to give him stick about it. But when I chatted with him and asked a few more questions I found out that actually he was very lonely and really struggling with homesickness. Kenny Jacket, Ian Holloway's assistant, pulled me aside one day after training and told me he liked how I cared about other players. For me that was a great compliment. Maybe I had learned something of what Keegan told me all those years before, 'As captain you need to give even more of yourself to the team.'

On April 2nd 2001 the club went into financial administration. Players' wages were not guaranteed. The future of this historic club was now unstable. Everyone involved – players and staff – were rocked. QPR was in my blood. I'd walked into the building as a fifteen-year-old nearly twenty years earlier. I had returned as a seasoned pro with several hundred league and cup games under my belt hoping to get them back in the Premier

League. But now at nearly thirty-four years old I was facing a relegation battle again. I felt the weight of the battle heavier than ever. Unfortunately, we lost the battle and were relegated three games before the end of the season at Huddersfield, where we lost 2-1. It was a must-win for both teams because we were both in the bottom three and the relegation zone. When a team is relegated, it is a result, not of one game, but of a long season, being worn down and getting into the habit of losing. Confidence is low. Players often start a game well but fade very quickly after going a goal down as belief visibly drains from the team. Resilience is lacking. You tend to feel half a yard slower. And you feel the pressure of the crowd, as boos and abuse become the weekly norm. Players become fearful and hesitant. You feel heaviness upon you as you enter each match. It takes character to go out and put in an honest performance in those circumstances.

We did our best but simply lacked enough confidence and quality on that day at Huddersfield. And I was partly at fault for their winning goal. I got hold of the ball in midfield around the halfway line. When the team is playing well and you look up, you may have four or five options of where to pass the ball. When the team is struggling, you are fortunate if you have even one. It's as if your own players disappear and ghost behind the opposition. As I controlled the ball, the options I'd seen before it came to me, all disappeared. In a split second I needed to decide. Do I just kick it forward aimlessly or do I try and manoeuvre the ball and look for an opening to one of my own players? I decided on the latter. It was a mistake. Nothing appeared for me. And now I was like an NFL quarterback twisting and turning to avoid being hunted down by the defensive line. In the end I was tackled. I think it was actually a foul, but the referee waved play on and the opposition burst forward onto our back four. Some poor defending followed, and we were 2-1 down – a score line that remained for the rest of the match.

It took me a long time, in fact the whole summer, to get over that defeat and the subsequent relegation. The sense of responsibility seemed greater now that I was senior player. Psychologically I was exhausted. My body ached from the accumulation of over 600 games. My right knee was swelling from time to time and needed to be carefully managed. And being the highest paid player at a club in financial administration, I was beginning to feel that my days were numbered at QPR.

Ian Holloway and I had played against each other. He was a young manager. I actually quite liked him. He was enthusiastic, an encourager, a bit quirky and he loved QPR, whom he'd served with great honour in his playing days. When he arrived, I think he probably didn't want me at the club for two reasons. First, I was our top wage earner and had a couple of years left on my contract. Ian would have realized he could get in two or three raw young players for my wages. Second, I was an influence in the dressing room and with the fans. Maybe he thought my presence would undermine his authority. But that was never my desire, nor would it ever be the case. But because of this, he didn't really entrust himself to me as his most senior player. I can understand this, and I respected Ian's way even if it wasn't what I preferred.

However, I came back for preseason training in the summer of 2001, super fit and ready to go. I scored in a 3-1 win in a friendly match against Chelsea. Then I received some surprise news. My mum and dad popped round to our house to see the grandchildren, Jake and Ava. By this time my father was back at Charlton in the Premier League as assistant manager to Alan Curbishley. Charlton's stadium, The Valley, was packed every week and the best players in the country were coming to town. Republic of Ireland international, Mark Kinsella, their midfield playmaker, was injured and set to be sidelined for a few months. So Curbishley asked my dad to find out if I'd be interested in coming on loan for three months. If I did well, Charlton would take over the rest of my contract at QPR. It was almost a replica of when my dad asked me to come to Gillingham, back in the 1980s. This was a win-win situation for me. For QPR it relieved them of my wages for a few months and maybe the next two years. For Charlton it filled a gap relatively cheaply. For me, it was a dream return to the Premier League at almost thirty-four, finally pulling on the red shirt of my dad's beloved Charlton Athletic, the team he made more appearances for than any other outfield player in their history. In fact, we are the only father and son to have ever both played for this historic club.

However, things didn't work out at Charlton in the way I had hoped. I only made five league appearances for them overall. I had no problem adjusting to the Premier League again, but injury struck and cut me down. I tore my calf muscle in training. I pushed off backwards in a practice match and felt like I'd been shot in the calf. It was bad. I had been extremely fortunate with injuries in my career: a few muscle strains, broken nose, sprained ankles, but at my age and with only a few weeks left on my loan period at Charlton I had it all to do to recover and prove I was worth a two-year contract. After many hours in the physio's room, in the gym and in the swimming pool, I returned to the first team squad and finished my loan spell fit. Because of the injury, Curbishley felt he couldn't sign me there and then but promised to look at things later in the season. Therefore, I returned to QPR and finished what turned out to be my final season as a professional footballer playing for the club where it all began.

We finished eighth in League Two. Ian Holloway was doing good things and like all good leaders was changing the culture and momentum for the good. We both hoped the Charlton loan deal would become permanent, but when that died, I knew I had to leave QPR. I had also developed a knee condition that needed rest in between games. I could have played for another couple of seasons, but I also wanted to finish my career when I was still playing well. Holloway knew this too and we had a difficult but inevitable meeting, which he summed up well in a 2011 article in the *Independent* newspaper about the hard task of letting players go:

> My toughest was Gavin Peacock at QPR. The fans loved him, he was a great lad, but he was also very highly paid and the club were in financial trouble. I knew I had to move him on and it was very awkward. All I could do was be honest and tell it how it was. I called him into my office and said, 'Look, Gav, you are thirty-four, you're having trouble with your knee – are you thinking about your long-term future?' I suggested a move into coaching. I was up front with him and, luckily for me, he didn't kick up a fuss.

I went home with a heavy heart after that meeting. I could have stayed at QPR and they were legally bound to honour my contract. But it wasn't the way I wanted to do things. It didn't seem honourable. I thought about a move somewhere else: a new start and a last hurrah with another club. I thought about coaching. Gerry Francis had suggested the same. But as I thought it through and discussed it with Amanda, it became clearer to me that the time was right for me to retire from the playing field. The book of Ecclesiastes says there is a time for everything:

> For everything there is a season, and a time for every matter under heaven: a time to be born, and a time to die; a time to plant, and a time to pluck up what is planted; a time to kill, and a time to heal; a time to break down, and a time to build up; a time to weep, and a time to laugh; a time to

mourn, and a time to dance; a time to cast away stones, and a time to gather stones together; a time to embrace, and a time to refrain from embracing; a time to seek, and a time to lose; a time to keep, and a time to cast away; a time to tear, and a time to sew; a time to keep silence, and a time to speak; a time to love, and a time to hate; a time for war, and a time for peace (Eccles. 3:1-8).

This was my time to retire from the game I loved. And in the late summer of 2002 I came to an agreement with QPR on my contract. They agreed to give me a testimonial match against Chelsea for my service to the club. So, after over 600 league and cup matches, 137 goals and 18 years as a professional, 10 of which were spent at Loftus Road, I finally hung up my boots. It was over. It was a strange thing to wake up the next day – the first morning since the summer of 1984 that I wasn't a professional footballer. I drove into the training ground one last time to say goodbye. I asked the youth team manager, Gary Waddock, if I could speak with the young players for a few minutes. Gary was an established first-team player when I joined QPR in the mid-80s, and we both knew how difficult it was to make it through the youth system at the club:

Lads, it seems like only yesterday I was sitting where you are now. So, make the most of this opportunity. You get the chance at something most boys can only dream of. So, play for the love of the game, not material benefits. Listen to Gary and learn. Work hard at your craft and don't give up. Then you'll have no regrets.

And that was it. I drove away from QPR's training ground for the last time with a lump in my throat, but an overwhelming sense of satisfaction and gratefulness. As I walked out of the building and into the car park, I looked and watched Ian Holloway and the players as they embarked on their morning warm-up. The buzz of the training ground continued. The laughter. The banter. The camaraderie. The thud of a leather boot on a leather ball. Life went on. QPR continued beyond me. And I joined a long line of ex-footballers who are now a small part of the history of the game. I was fifteen when I walked into the club and almost thirty-five when I left.

I think I had been the best player I could be with the talent I was given: a good player, but there were far better and more successful players than I. I had been through the full gamut of experiences in the game: promotion and relegation, cup finals and cup defeats, goals and injuries, the cheers and the jeers. I'd played in different countries around the world, with and against some of the best players in the world and for some of the best managers in the game. I had captained Newcastle, Chelsea and QPR, and led men into the arena. I'd been the boy that Bobby Robson describes, who inescapably fell in love with football as I watched my dad play and climbed the Valley terraces when I was small, and got to follow in his footsteps and into the beautiful game. And I saw that this game is more than what happens on Saturday from 3 pm – 4.45 pm. It's about people, their city and their team. It's about friendships and camaraderie and the hope of glory.

But all that glory doesn't last. Only God lasts. And God had blessed me, and I had been able to use my skills to honour Him in a small way and point to that. I'd testified to my faith in newspaper articles, magazines, TV and radio to the fact that there is a greater glory than football to be had. I had the unique opportunity to tell several footballers who Jesus was and how eternal life and joy is found in Him alone. We hosted the London Christian Footballers' Bible study. Christians in Sport printed out my Christian testimony on small leaflets, and Stuart Weir and I sent hundreds of signed tracts out to fans that wrote to me for autographs throughout the 1990s. I often wonder if one of those tracts was instrumental in someone coming to real faith in Jesus Christ. Then there was *Never Walk Alone*, the book I did with Alan Comfort. What was the point of my football career in summary? Simply this: a great opportunity and privilege to glorify and serve God. And this is true for any Christian in any walk of life.

Football is good but it is not God. Football is temporary: God is eternal.

9

A PUNDIT'S LIFE: FROM MATCH DAY TO 'MATCH OF THE DAY'

Starting again at age thirty-five is not easy. It's true that I had a good football career. But mine was not the era of £50,000 a week pay packets. I retired with a mortgage on my house and a need to work to provide for my wife and children. Work is part of being a responsible man. I had been in the workplace earning money from sixteen years old. So, there is a need to work to provide and a need to work to fulfil one's sense of responsibility. From the beginning of time, when God created the first man, He immediately called Adam to 'work and keep' the Garden of Eden (Gen. 2:15). Work is a good thing. It's not an easy thing but it is a good thing. That is why no one likes a lazy man who will not work. And that is also why men who desire to work but can't get a job for whatever reason often suffer greatly from a loss of purpose.

Starting again is a problem for many footballers. There are several reasons for this. Firstly, as I have already mentioned, their identity and sense of worth has been tied up in being a professional athlete. It's all they've ever thought about and all they've ever done since leaving school at maybe sixteen years old. Now it is gone, and they are still at a relatively young age. There is a void. Who are they now? Secondly, they have been paid for a job that most people pay money to play. Not many love their job. Yet a professional footballer has done something he loved, as difficult and costly as that has been. Thirdly, professional football is a high adrenaline job, which very few others can match. So, coming down from the weekly high of training and playing matches and settling into a less exhilarating work environment can be problematic. Finally, a man's marriage may come under strain. His wife has had a level of lifestyle that might not be sustainable after he retires. Her identity may have been tied up in his identity as a professional footballer. Of course, many women will marry the man for who he is and not the career he has. But even so, if she marries a professional footballer, football has shaped their lives powerfully. Now it is gone for her too. And if he cannot start again and regain his purpose and drive, she may lose respect for him. There are many factors that can lead to marital discord and divorce, but suffice to say there is reliable evidence that when footballers retire many of their marriages end.

For me, although I knew I wasn't immune to these things, I saw things differently. I knew I was made by God and saved by God to live for God, and that included work of whatever kind. It also meant that my identity wasn't tied to being a footballer but to being a Christian – a child of God. That could never change. It meant that I loved being a footballer but loved the Lord more, so adapting to 'normal' life wouldn't be insurmountable. You can't live on adrenaline forever no matter how thrilling the job may be. I also knew my marriage was not built on football but Jesus Christ. He was the foundation and that hadn't changed. My rock hadn't moved. So, I had some stability from which to start again.

This is not to say it was easy for me. I had considered the coaching and management track. With my father's management career and my leadership of the teams I played for, it seemed a natural course to take. But I was also being offered opportunities in the media. Capital Radio in London and BBC Radio 5 had approached me to start doing co-commentaries. I was also asked to fly to Singapore where they broadcast English Premier League football to millions in the East. So, for the first few months after I retired, I threw myself into learning the new trade.

Those trips to Singapore working under the direction of Andy Tait as my producer and the brilliant John Dykes as main presenter helped me hone my skills on live TV. Back home, I often used to do a fifteen-hour day on a Saturday for Capital Radio travelling to somewhere like Middlesbrough and back with my fellow commentator Andy Burton. Andy was a bright young talent with whom it was very easy to work. It wasn't lucrative, but I enjoyed my time with Capital and learned a lot. However, the BBC was a higher level and had far greater listening figures as a national station. The experienced broadcaster, Rob Knoffman, would have me listen back to my commentaries at TV Centre a few days after a match and instruct me on how I could improve. His tips were invaluable. For instance, there is a difference between saying, 'That's a great goal!' in regular face-to-face conversation and saying it on the radio, where no one can see you. You need to give it more emphasis, more 'oomph', when you are on air. You need to convey feeling and paint a picture with the tone of your voice, not just your words. You also need to develop your own style and rhythm so that your words have a certain cadence and even a lyrical quality. In that way you become unique and recognizable. Think of the best commentators or co-commentators and you'll know this to be true.

After my first nine months of doing a variety of media companies, the BBC was starting to become my staple. I worked hard; learning names of players from all divisions, learning names of players from international leagues, working at the drop of a hat when an opportunity arose or if a regular on the BBC team dropped out and there was a gap to fill. I discussed with Amanda the need to make sacrifices in the early stages of this new career and that it would be easier as things progressed.

Doing BBC 5 Live matches on radio also meant that the BBC TV producers and programme editors heard me. My big break on TV came when a BBC editor named Lance Hardy approached me to be on the main panel with former Tottenham Hotspur legend and BBC media stalwart, Garth Crooks, ex-Crystal Palace and Sheffield Wednesday striker, Mark Bright, and my old Newcastle United team-mate, Andy Cole, for the Africa Cup of Nations in 2004. The tournament went well for me, and I was immediately invited for an appearance on the prestigious Saturday lunchtime magazine show, *Football Focus*, and the Saturday afternoon results show, *Final Score*. It was nerve wracking for sure. Going live on air in front of several million people and knowing that when you speak it's your face and voice alone on that screen where mistakes cannot be covered is quite daunting. I worked with Ray Stubbs, a real gentleman and a great professional. Ray was a tremendous anchorman; making everything look easy, putting his pundits at ease and acting cool under pressure. Lance Hardy edited both *Football Focus* and *Final Score*. When you start any new career you need someone to believe in your talent. It's always a risk giving someone a chance in the TV business, because your own reputation as an editor is at stake. So, I will always be grateful for Lance, who also became a good friend.

At that time, I watched more football than ever. I recorded games and watched them as homework. I read the newspapers avidly and researched all the teams across the leagues. Then I observed how experienced pundits like ex-Liverpool pair, Mark Lawrenson and Alan Hansen, did it. They were the two top men when I arrived on the scene and they were on all the prime-time BBC football shows along with ex-England captain Alan Shearer. Hansen had a unique gravitas on air and was able to boil down his analysis to memorable, concise phrases. But he gave me one tip I'll always remember when I asked him, 'Alan, what's the secret to success in this business?' 'Gav', he answered, 'it's not what you say, as much as how you say it!!' That was okay for him to say with his deep Scottish 'Sean Connery' accent. But I got the gist and began to work on my personal style and link phrases.

Lawrenson was a really good all-round broadcaster. He could do radio or TV co-commentaries or studio analysis. And unlike Hansen who mainly stayed on the Premier League and international matches, 'Lawro' had lines on every club across the leagues and an interest in football's current affairs in all aspects of the game. He was personally very encouraging to me. I observed his skill when we were live on air. We would often have thirty seconds to fill before the end of *Football Focus* and Ray Stubbs would throw a last question at him. With only seconds to speak, Lawro had the ability to pull out a short one liner with a turn of phrase that was either funny or poignant. I began to think how I would answer in that circumstance given the task.

One of the key things to master on TV is the ability to give timely and succinct answers. There is a running order for the show, which includes the presenters' opening lines and link lines, the different pieces of VT (video transmission) and the spaces for chat and analysis. If you take too long to say something, you put the running order out of joint. Then the editors have to work furiously to chop time out of other areas and may even lose an important video piece or a coach's interview from the programme. This speaking skill isn't easy to grasp, especially if English is your second language. It was definitely the case for

Peter Schmeichel. He was as commanding a presence on screen as he was as a player on the field, but the former Manchester United and Danish international took too long to say things. Consequently, he didn't last that long as a regular BBC analyst.

Another key skill I learned early in my TV career was how to work with an earpiece. Many people don't like this, because when the earpiece is in you hear everything that is going on in the editor's suite: director, producer and voices galore. When you are on set and trying to answer a question and a host of other people are talking in your ear, and not always to you, it can be really distracting. You need to develop your 'editorial brain', that is the ability to listen to two conversations at once. If you conquer this, it is gold dust. All of a sudden you don't feel in the dark when on air. You feel safer. You hear your producer or director giving you information. Talk could be going on, on set, but I would hear in my earpiece, 'Ray, ask Gavin about Chelsea's strikers for your next question. And Gavin you have thirty seconds on the answer.'

This gave Ray Stubbs a chance to think of his question and it gave me a chance to think of my answer. Then when I was actually giving the answer, I would have someone counting down in my ear,

Me: 'So the reason Chelsea have scored so many this season...'

Earpiece: 'Gavin, out in 10, 9, 8...'

Me: '...is that both their strikers...'

Earpiece: '7, 6, 5, 4...'

Me: '...have remained...'

Earpiece: '3...'

Me: '...fit...'

Earpiece: '2...'

Me: '...all...'

Earpiece: ' ...1'

Me: '…season'

Earpiece: '…and out. Well done, Gavin. Ray, now introduce the Liverpool VT, looking at Camera 3.'

People find it amazing when they hear all this is going on in your ear whilst the studio presentation that they receive at home through their television sets is calm and peaceful. Working with an earpiece was actually very helpful after mastering the ability to use it. It helped me to be able to take direction and know where we were going in the show. It also gives the editor a chance to make corrections or feed his pundits statistical information. A good editor is able to keep an eye on the big picture and the camera angles he wants to use, but he is also listening very carefully to the on-screen conversation. For instance, and this happens often, I might be making a comment like this: 'David Beckham was excellent again today for Manchester United. He was everywhere on the pitch and scored again – his…' And my mind would go blank on how many goals Beckham has scored that season. The editor sees this slight pause and feeds a line in the ear, 'Tenth goal this season.' And as he says it in my ear, I repeat on air, '…his tenth goal this season.' I look good and the show is producing accurate content for the audience, thus serving the BBC mission statement: 'To act in the public interest, serving all audiences through the provision of impartial, high-quality and distinctive output and services which inform, educate and entertain.'

It doesn't always go as planned, however. In fact, when you are doing live TV, you must be prepared for the unexpected. One evening as we were half an hour from going live with *Match of the Day*, the air conditioning in the studio broke. It was a hot day in late August anyway, but add that to the huge amount of studio lighting and no cool air, and the place became a furnace very quickly. Huge fans were brought in as we approached airtime. Ray Stubbs was presenting, and I was next to Lee Dixon as one of two pundits. The trouble was, as I sat there I began to sweat and the studio was simply getting hotter. I had no hair to hide the beads of sweat forming on my head and beginning to drip down my face. I was frantically dabbing myself with a tissue and the thought of being live in front of several million people in two minutes only made me perspire more profusely.

When the signature *Match of the Day* theme tune ends, the presenter usually introduces the show and the two pundits, who stay on a wide camera angle. Then he takes it straight into the first highlights package of the first match. At that point we can rest in the studio and regroup. 'Ray! Whatever you do, don't ask me a question before we get to the first highlights package. If you ask me anything the camera is going to zoom in on a close up. And I'm looking like I've been swimming!' I said this with sweat now running down my face. 'Let's get to the highlights and the make-up lady will be able to sort out my head!' Within moments we were on air live, with music playing and lights at full blast and full heat!

> Welcome to *Match of the Day*. We have a thrilling show for you tonight packed with goals. We go to Stamford Bridge for Chelsea's all London battle with Arsenal. Before we go there, with us in the studio is ex-Arsenal and England defender, Lee Dixon and ex-Chelsea captain, Gavin Peacock. I'm not telling you the result, but Gavin's smile may give you a clue!

And the camera panned in on my face, with me now trying to force an awkward smile into the lens whilst sweat dripped off my chin and onto the table in front of me! I looked like I had just played in the match myself!

I knew I wasn't the biggest name to hit the BBC Football screens. My stats, which would often appear underneath my face on screen at the beginning of each show, paled into insignificance next to someone like Lee Dixon with multiple England appearances and Premier League championships to his credit. So, I knew I needed to be extra good at my job. I didn't want to say the obvious on screen. The fans are more educated than ever on football because of the vast media coverage and expert analysis today. Therefore, they need to be fed insight as to why something has happened, or they want an observation of an important detail of the game they might have missed but a professional eye can see. I also knew that my judgement calls needed to be sound, especially with TV appearances. On the radio, if you make a call on a live game no one can see if you got the name of the player wrong or if indeed you got the call wrong. But on TV it's there for all to observe. Nevertheless, the standard expected on the BBC, radio or TV, was very high. Starting this new career involved a lot of work.

If I were to sum up things that you need to succeed in starting again from scratch in any career it would be:

1. Have a clear vision of where you want to go and what you need to do to achieve it. This might involve some tweaks along the way, but it will stay mainly fixed.

2. Remember that no one owes you anything. Just because you have achieved some success in the past, it doesn't mean people will or should make it easy for you in the future.

3. Learn quickly and adapt to new things well. This can be more difficult the older you get and when your brain isn't as agile as in younger years.

4. Take correction humbly. You're going to make mistakes, and others will tell you so if they care about you or the business.

5. Observe those more experienced than you in this new career and imitate what they do.

6. Aim to succeed and be willing to fail in trying. Every new start comes with risk. Don't be afraid to fail.

7. Focus on producing excellence for others, not just yourself.

8. Persevere.

***

By the summer of 2004 I had made the BBC broadcast team for the European Championships in Portugal, where I did a mixture of TV and radio. Big international tournaments are an incredible experience to broadcast. The cream of world football is on show and the world comes to watch. It's colourful, thrilling and exhausting. I wasn't on the biggest games. That was left to the A team: main presenter, Gary Lineker, and main pundits Alan Hansen, Ian Wright and Alan Shearer. But there were plenty of other matches, newsfeeds and programmes going on. The tournament dossier I received was huge. The research that went into it took months. Every team was profiled with information and statistics on every player in the tournament. The commentators have the hardest job. Imagine the names involved in a game between Greece and Russia! I worked with excellent broadcasters and commentators like Jonathan Pearce, Simon Brotherton, John Murray, Steve Wilson, Guy Mowbray, Alan Green and the inimitable John Motson amongst others. I also watched the emergence of the very gifted Jacqui Oatley, the first female commentator on *Match of the Day*.

In fact, I worked with many gifted men and women at the BBC. They called the pundits, the presenters, and the commentators 'The Talent'. But I would argue that the big talent lay behind the scenes: from the editors and directors to the people who put together the video pieces for the highlight shows, to the camera and sound workers, to the logistics men and women, to the ladies who did our make-up. (Yes, I needed anti-shine powder on my head!) The BBC Football folks were a real team, and that's one of the things I loved about working with them.

After the Euros, we took a family holiday to Canada for the first time. We spent time in Vancouver, British Columbia, and Banff, Alberta, in the Rocky Mountains. We enjoyed Canada and for the following few years made it a regular holiday destination. But at that time in 2004 we didn't know that Canada was to play a big part in our lives to come. That holiday was also the occasion of a strange encounter. I was eating breakfast with Amanda, Jake and Ava in our hotel overlooking the water and watching the cruise liners come by, when I heard a familiar voice call my name. It was John Motson, Britain's most famous commentator and my BBC colleague. He and his wife were on an Alaskan cruise and had just stopped for a few hours for breakfast in Vancouver. John was extremely influential at the BBC and told me that the powers that be were very pleased with my work in Portugal. That was a great boost. John had also been commentating when my father played and was the son of a Methodist minister. He was sympathetic to my Christian faith and he supported and encouraged me greatly in my TV and radio career.

For the next few years things went from strength to strength for me at the BBC. I was a regular on BBC 5 Live, *Football Focus*, *Final Score* and *Match of the Day*. *Match of the Day* is the BBC's flagship and most prestigious football programme. It first aired in 1964 and is the longest-running football television programme in the world. Former Arsenal and England player Lee Dixon and I also forged a great partnership on *Match of the Day 2* with Adrian Chiles as our presenter. Adrian was one of the most talented presenters I ever worked with. He was so quick witted and extremely casual at the same time. He had presented radio and TV daytime programmes on all manner of issues – business, politics and sport. He was very well read – a highly intelligent man. However, although he was a big West Bromwich Albion fan, he made out that he knew nothing about football (which was somewhat true!). This was the opposite of Gary Lineker on *Match of the Day*, who had been one of the best players of his time for Tottenham Hotspur and England. When Gary asked the pundits a question, he already knew the answer. When Adrian asked, you knew he didn't know anything. But he was a sensational broadcaster, and this was his trick. Because of Adrian, *Match of the Day 2* had a little more comedy involved even though the football analysis was still very serious.

Adrian's chemistry with Lee and me worked well and our show was very popular. Editor-in-Chief for the programme, Mark Demuth, was an astute leader. He gave me a platform on MOTD2 and helped me improve my TV presence and skills. Talking over VT is very difficult because you need to get clear points across without falling behind the video play. Mark helped me with simple tips like writing down a good opening line into the video and a strong line to get out of the video. We were also tasked with putting together tactical pieces for the show. I enjoyed being involved in this aspect of creativity. Making a successful programme, which the audience loves, is a thrill.

Let me give you an insight into a show like *Match of the Day* or *Match of the Day 2*. The shows go out live in the evening, but the work takes all day. We would arrive at midday and watch all the games at once on multiple screens. The editor would designate one particular game for me and my fellow pundit to each keep a special watch on. We knew those games would be heavily featured in the show at night – so we needed to know what was going on. But we still had to look across all the games because we would need to make comment on them. I would have one of the guys from the backroom with me. I then looked for patterns to emerge in my 'focus game'. Let's say Chelsea were playing Manchester United and Frank Lampard was playing well, and Chelsea were winning. I would tell my man to mark down time codes on Lampard's good play whenever I called them out. Simultaneously, I looked for the tactical reason why Chelsea were winning the game and I would have those time codes marked down too. I was actually working on two analysis pieces for the show: one player focus and one tactical analysis. All this whilst keeping an eye on every other match as well.

At the end of the games, around 4.45 pm, I had perhaps thirty different time codes on my 'focus' game. Gary Lineker or whoever the presenter was would begin to write his script for the evening show. The interviews from team managers around the country would start to come into TV Centre and the programme editor would begin to write the running order. Meanwhile, I would go upstairs to the edit suite and work with the tech guys on making my time-coded clips into an edifying sixty-second piece of VT for each of my analysis pieces, player focus and tactical analysis. The next couple of hours were spent deciding on the main message of the pieces and working out the best clips to use: then there was the use of slow motion, freezes, arrows and circles to demonstrate the tactical point – all coming together in a one-minute end product for each analysis piece. During the evening show I would talk over each piece in turn as it was played on air live. I enjoyed the creativity involved in this facet of the job.

After finishing work on my particular video pieces, I would look at the main running order and start to think of lines and comments I would make on all the games and players. We may have some particular talking points slated for discussion, usually involving refereeing decisions. So, I would often phone or text my friend Keith Hackett for advice. Keith was the General Manager of Professional Game Match Officials and widely regarded as one of the best referees of all time. It is all too easy to criticize referees. Sometimes you need to understand things from their perspective. Keith was a good source of help here.

When all this was done, there were usually a couple of hours to rest, eat and prepare before going on air live at 10.30 pm. We might also have a guest manager or current player appearing with us on the show, who would turn up in that time. It was always an education if Gordon Strachan, David Moyes or Alex McLeish were on the show. They were encyclopaedic in their knowledge of the game. About an hour before airtime we would go into make-up and get changed. The nerves would start to build. I usually arrived on set fifteen minutes beforehand, adjust my earpiece to make sure I had good communication with the gallery and get my notes in order on the table in front of me. Then countdown would begin, lights were dimmed, the iconic *Match of the Day* theme tune would play and then in my ear I would hear, 'Five, four, three, two, one...we are live on *Match of the Day*!' Lights on! On air in front of five or six million people! It's strange but I never thought about the numbers after a while. It was just a discussion on football – the beautiful game that I loved. It was a dream second career.

Speaking of guests who appeared on our shows, one stands out above all and that was Tony Blair who was at that time the Prime Minister of the United Kingdom. The show was *Football Focus*. I was in the studio for *Final Score* that day and wasn't on the actual programme with him. But the level of security at TV Centre was immense; police swarmed the building. Sniffer dogs were everywhere. Four advisers surrounded Mr Blair as he walked into the football green room. It was election year and he was using the programme to show the public he was a true football fan. However, I didn't realize that he was a Newcastle United supporter and had watched me play in my time at St James' Park. He had a few brief words with me when he came off set and then he was whisked away by his officials and security team. It was surreal. It's not every day you go to work and meet the PM!

By 2006, my BBC career was in full flow and growing stronger. I was appearing on *Match of the Day, Match of the Day 2, Football Focus, Final Score*, and the *African Cup of Nations*. I was also regularly commentating on matches for BBC 5 Live at Premier League stadiums all over England and appearing on a variety of other 5 Live shows. Add to that midweek magazine shows and interviews for magazines, and life was busy. In addition, I was asked to be male studio pundit for the England women's football. Celina Hinchcliffe was the presenter. She was a talented but unassuming young woman who was given the opportunity to spearhead a new era in TV coverage of women's football. Gabby Logan was the queen of female football presenters and Celina had the difficult task of following in her footsteps. She showed a few early nerves, but it was a delight to work with Celina and to see her emerge on screen and in 2006 become the first woman to present *Football Focus*.

At this time, women's football was beginning to gain a greater following. The BBC and editor Lance Hardy can take a lot of credit for platforming it. Now young women don't just look at David Beckham or Ryan Giggs or Cristiano Ronaldo as role models; they look to Faye White, Rachel Brown, Eniola Aluko, Sue Smith, Alex Scott and England women's greatest ever goal-scorer, Kelly Smith. Most of these women appeared next to me in the studio at some point. All of them showed integrity and intelligence as they spoke about the game. It's inspiring to see how the women's game has grown over the past fifteen years. Realistically, it will never surpass the men's game in terms of a spectacle of power and skill and won't get the same viewing figures. But it's women's football – a game in its own right – and in its own right is a growing sport, influencing and encouraging many young girls to love and to play the game. My own daughter, Ava, played football in school and beyond, and is a good amateur player today. Watching her play is always a great thrill for me. She's fast, skilful and can get a goal – just like her dad!

At this point of my media career my national profile was even higher than when I was playing football. My face was on TV screens in front of millions of people weekly. My voice was on the radio airwaves. I was also getting asked to appear at several charity events or emcee prestigious business events. Yet despite all of this, I didn't think I would be doing it for a long time. I couldn't put my finger on it. I absolutely loved my second career and couldn't easily see myself doing anything else. Nevertheless, that nagging thought was always in the back of my mind.

**

The 2006 World Cup in Germany was the next big platform and it was sensational. I had never even been to a World Cup before, and being based in Berlin for a few weeks meant being at the epicentre of the football world. The crowds, the colours, the culture and the cream of world football talent were all-consuming. I did a mix of TV studio appearances and radio and TV live commentaries as well. This meant I saw some of the rest of Germany as I travelled to stadiums in Cologne and Kaiserslautern as well as broadcasting in Berlin and the BBC TV centre where we set up. Through the window in the BBC studio loomed the Berlin Quadriga on top of the Brandenburg

Gate. This impressive statue of a carriage drawn by four horses was designed in 1793. It was seized by Napoleon and taken to Paris, returned in 1814, and barely survived World War II. It spoke of the history of the place in which this great tournament was being played.

Working at a World Cup isn't all glamour though. It's actually exhausting. There are so many games and so much going on around the matches, and things are changing all the time. So, you are relentlessly studying the matches and having to keep up to date with news in between the games so that you are well prepared when broadcasting. Then there is the travel to different games around the country, arriving at the stadium three hours before kick-off and leaving two hours after. And finally, there is the pressure of broadcasting on the BBC at the World Cup where viewing figures skyrocket. Nevertheless, it was a platform to be enjoyed and the view was great. Not only did the best players in the world come to an event like this, the best ex-players in the world come. The BBC team stayed at a lovely boutique hotel set just off the main Unter den Linden, which ran through the middle of Berlin all the way to the Brandenburg Gate. One morning John Motson, Mark Lawrenson and I went for a run together. When we returned to the hotel, we saw Brazilian triple World Cup winning legend and possibly the best player who ever lived, Pelé, having a cup of coffee with Gary Lineker. Lineker had an A-List group of friends!

My mind drifted back to a day in the summer of 1978 when I was living in the USA as a young kid and went to a 'soccer' camp that Pelé was conducting. He was playing for the New York Cosmos in the NASL (North American Soccer League) at the time, trying to kick-start football fever in the States. I ran onto the pitch at the end of his session and fought my way through the crowd of youngsters surrounding him and asking for autographs. All I wanted to do was touch the great man. I squeezed between two bigger boys and then, for just a moment, Pelé turned and looked at me, smiled and held out his hand. I returned mine quickly and clasped his. I'd met my hero! In an instant I was quickly shoved aside as others pressed in. And Pelé disappeared from my view surrounded by a sea of young fans. But that was a moment I never forgot. I don't think I washed my right hand for a week afterwards. However, Pelé's example was also something I always remembered: the importance of looking people in the eye when they ask for an autograph or handshake and how much a simple smile means to young fans. We should never neglect to learn from those kinds of moments in life.

***

After returning from Germany and the World Cup I continued in my normal routine with the BBC but was asked to present a couple of Radio 5 Live documentary pieces and a few chat shows. Presenting is a different skill in itself and something I was keen to learn. I also asked the football editors if I could present a piece for *Football Focus* on Christianity in football. They said 'No', but I could do something on religion in football. I agreed and interviewed players from Jewish, Muslim and Christian backgrounds. It was well received when it was broadcast. On the day, I sat on the *Football Focus* set with Jake Humphrey presenting and Mark Lawrenson and former Arsenal and England defender Martin Keown. Certainly, the Premiership had become much more multi-cultural and global by then and this introduced players with various faiths. My friend and fellow Christian, Linvoy Primus, gave a very winsome interview, and I received many emails from football fans who were very encouraged by what they saw and heard. It's good to see how Linvoy has grown in his spiritual leadership and is now Head of Professionals at Christians in Sport with Graham Daniels as General Director.

Outside of football I began to present *Songs of Praise* on BBC One, the UK's longest-running Christian-based TV show. A highlight was filming in Spain's Costa del Sol in the setting of Fuengirola Castle, with Christian singer/songwriter, Graham Kendrick, leading the hymns. It was like open-air church and hundreds of folks were singing within the castle walls. It was pre-recorded and I needed to do links to the camera in between songs. On one link I was up in one of the castle turrets and I couldn't get my lines out properly. I kept getting it wrong, take after take. The pressure of having a castle full of people waiting and eagerly looking up at me from below only added to my tongue-tiedness!

At this point I was turning down work because I was so busy. One Sunday I strangely appeared on two TV channels at the same time. I was live on BBC Two with the *African Cup of Nations* and I was also on BBC One presenting an episode of *Songs of Praise*, which we had pre-recorded a few weeks before.

***

Things were great in my new career, but change was on the horizon. Towards the end of 2006 Amanda became very ill and spent a week in hospital with a severe kidney infection. During this time, the doctors found something suspicious on one of her ovaries and suspected possible ovarian cancer. Suffering often recalibrates one's focus. The most important person in my life was in a health crisis and nothing else mattered. At the same time, I began to throw myself into reading the Bible and prayer to an increased degree. One morning I was reading from a passage in the New Testament where the Apostle Paul talks about preaching the Word for the future of Christianity. It read: 'I charge you in the presence of God and of Christ Jesus, who is to judge the living and the dead, and by his appearing and his kingdom: preach the word; be ready in season and out of season; reprove, rebuke, and exhort, with complete patience and teaching' (2 Tim. 4: 1-2).

Something inside me stirred. 'What a thing this is!', I thought, 'I wonder if this is something I am called to do.' To preach God's Word and be a pastor to people is a weighty task. I thought of my beloved wife in the hospital bed and the fragility and brevity of life. I thought of how I had enjoyed being a leader in my football career, mentoring younger players and that particular time when I addressed the men during a moment of crisis during our relegation battle at QPR. And I thought of how I had been trained these past few years in the art of communication, and yet still felt it wouldn't be a long career. Consequently, I began another switch of fields: a switch that had gone from the pitch to punditry and now to the pulpit...with a move across an ocean to boot! It was tough to succeed on the pitch and in punditry. But I was now about to enter the hardest season of my life.

10

SWITCHING FIELDS: A PREACHER'S CALL

'You'll be a preacher one day, Gavin.' These were the words of my good friend, the Reverend Tony Roake, who had been my spiritual mentor since I was twenty-one and newly married in Bournemouth. Even though I had chosen the media for my next career, Tony saw something I didn't. We would talk about family life, football and faith as we met for a monthly lunch in a quaint village near Wisley just off Junction 11 of the M25 motorway. And one day Tony came out with what I thought was a wild prediction about preaching. 'No way, Tony', I replied. I was happy giving my testimony at churches and telling youngsters the good news of what God has done for people through Jesus and the hope they can have in Him. But I never thought about being a leader in the church. I must admit I dismissed it out of hand and Tony wisely did not press the issue.

Then came that moment when Amanda was ill, and I was reading that particular Bible passage, and something lit up in my heart. But this was an internal, subjective feeling. I could have been wrong. I discussed my thoughts with Amanda and then went to see my leadership in our church at the time, St Michael's Anglican Church in Wilmington, Kent. The vicar,

Richard Arding, affirmed some giftings and spiritual leadership. He said he would give me some opportunities to preach and that I should also do some preliminary Old Testament and New Testament studies at Ridley Hall in Cambridge. He also indicated that a person should only enter ministry if they fulfil certain character qualifications laid out in the Bible. It was indeed a high calling.

So, in the September of 2007, twenty-three years after leaving Bexley Grammar, I went back to school. I found the academics stimulating and stretching at the same time. I was not used to reading thick books on theology and writing 4,000-word papers with footnotes and references. I couldn't even type. Twice a week I drove one hour north of London to leafy Cambridge City and the beautiful Ridley Hall grounds. You could smell the history in the place. I was situated very close to Trinity College where the famous Court Run would take place, a race that was depicted in the film *Chariots of Fire*. I was still working for the BBC however, and found myself studying with men preparing for ministry that were huge football fans.

They were very keen to talk about football and the comments I'd made on games at the weekend on TV. I would answer their questions and converse with them about their favourite teams, but deep down I just wanted to study the Bible! My time at Cambridge simply affirmed my desire to pursue full-time ministry. And it wasn't long after I began my studies that I sat down with my wife and dropped the bombshell, 'Amanda, I think I'm going to give it all up and take some time to prepare for this task. And I wonder what it would look like to go away somewhere where people don't know me and wouldn't be tempted to confuse the football player and BBC pundit with the pastor. We know Canada well now, and we've got a small holiday home there. What about moving abroad for a few years so I can complete my studies? It would be a great adventure but also a great test of character for us all.'

This was a huge decision. We had a great life and we were extremely happy. We lived in a very nice house close to our extended family. Our children were in good schools and had lots of friends. I earned good money in a second dream career, which seemed only to be growing more successful. People would think I was foolish to give it up. Family would be devastated and maybe not fully understand the reasons we were leaving. My wife brought up several other potential problems. Plus, I was asking her yet again to move, not around the corner but 5,000 miles away to a place where we didn't know a soul. And so we began a period of discussion and prayer, wrestling with the biggest decision of our lives. After many weeks and months of soul searching the decision was made. I needed to step up and initiate the final push to decide. But my wife, as always, was by my side and ready to show the faith and fortitude that makes her one in a million.

Our children were fifteen (Jake) and twelve (Ava) at the time we put the idea to them. These are not easy ages to move with children. Jake was in the prestigious Colfes – a private school in South East London. Ava was at one of the best girls' schools in the south of England – Dartford Grammar (the boys' school was made famous by the fact that Mick Jagger was a former student). We wanted them to be involved with this process and see how we made the decision for God-centred reasons. We weren't going for money. The reality was that according to Canadian law I wouldn't be able to earn anything for three years on a student visa. This was going to cost us financially. And after that a pastor's salary is not very much. We talked to the children and wanted them to see that they could not rely on anything in this life above God: not family, friends, or schools.

'These things are good, but they can all be taken away. God will never leave you wherever you go', we would say.

Our kids were amazing. I think they trusted our judgement and felt secure in our love for them, which stemmed from love for God and love for each other. They knew that things would be tough, but they had never been coddled so, not without a few tears or fears, they were up for the challenge. I knew this move would only strengthen them further. Breaking the news to parents and siblings was not at all easy and was met with great sadness and grief. We are a close family. My parents lived ten minutes away from us; so too my sister, Lauren, Andy her husband and Celine and Shania, our lovely nieces. Our neighbours, Nick and Jacqui Johnston, and their son, Thomas, were the best we had ever had. And Amanda's mother, Mary, lived close too. She spent much of her time with us and was a wonderful mother and grandmother. It probably hit her the hardest as she must have felt her world was falling apart.

Part of good decision-making is to consider the impact of your choice on circles of people around you. We did this of course. But I'm not sure I was prepared for how deep the wound would be for all of us. It was like an amputation and I felt very responsible for causing it. We then began to tell friends. Friends in our church whom we'd known for over a dozen years; and friends in the football world like Mark and Julie Stimson with whom we'd been through so much. On top of that I now needed to announce it to my colleagues and bosses at the BBC. Once word got out, my phone rang off the hook. Everyone wanted a line from me or an interview. It was an interesting and unusual story and would make for good reading. Newspapers and columns and websites were making their own comments, but I decided to do one personal interview with *The Times*. My friend and former Chelsea team-mate, Tony Cascarino, had a popular weekly column with them. I knew Tony would present my story with the utmost integrity and he did.

I was working for the BBC, studying at Cambridge and guiding my family into a move abroad with all the relational and logistical difficulties that come with it. I sorted out a seminary in Calgary, Alberta. We had our holiday home an hour outside the city in a town of eleven thousand people called Canmore. This was a big change from suburban London. We found schools for the children. Then we needed to rent our house in Wilmington in Kent, find movers who would take some of our furniture and possessions abroad and store the rest. Amanda did a huge amount of research and planning. Even small things like getting our two dogs immunized and paying for them to be on the same plane as us all took time and energy. One friend who came through in a time of need was my financial adviser, Nick Carew-Gibbs. Nick had been a prudent adviser over the years and had become one of those people upon whom you could always rely. He helped with many of the things one doesn't even think about with a move across seas. He is to this day one of my most trusted friends.

My last gig with the BBC was the Euros in Switzerland and Austria in June. I said my farewells in person and also live on air. I had made good friends in my six years working with these people. As I returned from the event, I felt a mixture of sadness at leaving my job and colleagues, and excitement at the prospect of a new challenge. But I also felt a huge pressure on me. The next few weeks went in a blur and the day finally came to leave the shores of the UK for Calgary, Alberta, in Canada. It was the 15th July 2008.

***

The morning of our departure is here. I am weighed down with the pressure. The past few months have taken their toll, physically, emotionally and spiritually. The house is virtually empty. The removal company has taken the lot. Our renters will be in next week. The kids are excited. Amanda looks apprehensive. Leaving her mum will be hard. My sister arrives with my nieces to say goodbye. Our next-door neighbours, Nick, Jacqui and Thomas are at the door now. Butterflies in the stomach. It feels like a match day in that sense. I look around the house and out into the beautiful woodland in which we live. 'What am I doing?'

My parents arrive. They will drive one car to the airport. Amanda's father, Mick, will take the dogs in his. My mother, Lesley, grabs a private moment with me. She bursts into tears. It feels like a knife is stuck in my heart and won't shift, leaving the feeling of a band of pain wrapped around it. The ache is deep. I know I'm crushing the person who gave me life. 'I have to do this mum.' She nods, 'I know, son.' Tears flow as we drive away. I look back at my mother-in-law, neighbours and my sister and nieces. The drive to Heathrow takes too long. The tension is too much. We arrive and walk into the airport. I'm by my father's side. 'It's like history repeating itself', he says, his voice cracking slightly as clearly he remembers all those years ago when he took us to live in Florida and that tearful goodbye with his own father, my grandad Tom. The ache in my chest persists.

We say our goodbyes. I'm trying to hold it together for the sake of my wife and children. I look at Jake and Ava. They can't fully appreciate the gravity of what is happening. More hugs and tears and then we are off, through security, into the waiting lounge and onto a plane bound for Calgary and the Canadian Rockies. The kids are looking forward to the new life ahead. They have their fears, but they are adaptable. My wife has mixed feelings. She must make yet another home. But homemaking is written deep in her DNA as a woman. We've already had sixteen different addresses in our married life, and she has, with skill and wisdom, made each place warm and comfortable, no matter how long we lived there. Now a new challenge is before her in a new country without the support of her wider family or circle of friends.

I feel the burden of leadership in all of this. Though deep down I know it is the right thing and I know God will provide, I also realize the pain it is causing and will cause those I love most deeply. At forty years old I am also leaving the country I love and have represented in the sports arena. I am leaving a job I love and the game of football which is woven into the fabric of our society, so that having played it professionally and broadcast professionally, I feel connected to the British public in a profound way. The ache inside my chest won't go away. I think it might always be there to some degree.

I drift off to sleep on the plane and, after what seems like minutes, awaken to the pilot's voice announcing our landing. I look out of the window and see the spectacular Rocky Mountains below. I've seen them many times before but now they will be my home. Who would have thought that this boy from South East of England would make a pioneering move to a small Rocky Mountain town? I've swapped BBC stardom for anonymity in Canada; stadiums and studios for seminary study; financial security for living on our savings. I remember the comforting words of 1 Samuel 2:30: 'For those who honour me I will honour.' The ache in my chest subsides slightly. The plane touches down. We arrive in our new land.

***

Even though Canada has similarities to the UK, being primarily English speaking and a Commonwealth country with the same Queen, it has its own culture. And we were strangers and sojourners who needed to adapt to that. For one thing, the humour is slightly different. We do far more sarcasm in the

UK! My son was inadvertently offending his school friend by making fun of his new sweater. 'He is upset, dad. In England all my mates would do this. It means they like you!'

Of course, everything is new in another country like Canada and you find yourself constantly learning. You are the foreigner on someone else's land. You start over again. You need to navigate your way around a new town or city. You need to buy new clothes for a new environment. You need to adjust to a new environment. Yes, there is the pristine beauty of mountains and lakes, and there is also the morning surprise when you find a 500 lb elk in your back yard or encounter a grizzly bear on a walking trail! This is slightly different to bumping into foxes in the streets of suburban London. You must also learn new systems and ways of doing things for everything, including paying household bills and healthcare. You need two sets of tyres for your car in Canada: summer and winter. Speaking of which, you need to learn to cope with the weather. This was perhaps the most difficult thing. Within a few months winter had arrived, and temperatures were diving to minus thirty degrees. That's brutal, like nothing I'd ever experienced.

So, I found myself driving into Calgary several times a week in extreme cold and snow to study Greek and Hebrew as I embarked upon my theological studies in seminary. I felt like everything was being stretched and tested: my role as a husband and father, my intellect, my character and above all, my faith. When everything you can be tempted to rely on is stripped back, you find out what kind of ground you stand on, what you believe and where your hope is. I had trusted in Jesus Christ as my Lord and Saviour from age eighteen. Now I was preparing for church ministry, and a further refinement was necessary. I not only needed to know more about God through my studies, I needed to know the reality of God in a deeper way in my life. Just like physical fitness always comes through an element of pain and discomfort, so it is with spiritual fitness. All my family grew in faith in those first few years. We saw God provide for us materially. We also saw God provide for us spiritually through the church we went to in Banff, the town next door to Canmore and their faithful minister, Norm Derkson. Norm also gave me opportunities to exercise spiritual leadership through preaching regularly and leading men's groups and community groups.

Over the next few years, we sold our UK residence and bought a bigger house in Canada. As each season passed, the homesickness became less intense and we began to build history and memories in Canada. The children settled more quickly than Amanda and me, but of course they were less entrenched in English life and culture than we were. However, even having been here more than a decade, there is not a day that goes by when my mind does not think of England and all that it means to me. The ache in my chest remains, some days it's almost imperceptible, but it's always there.

In 2011, I finished my Masters Studies and our three-year visas were coming to an end. I began to speak with churches in the UK and several were interested in me being their pastor. But either the conversation didn't continue, or I felt it wasn't the right fit for me. Time was ticking away, and we were looking at the possibility of returning to our mother country when events took another twist and turn.

I received a message on Twitter one Saturday evening from a Calgary pastor named Clint Humfrey. He was out in Banff for the weekend with his wife and children and asked me to recommend a church. I recommended ours. Clint walked into the church the next morning wearing a ten-gallon hat, boots and a belt buckle that was bigger than the Community Shield.[1]

---

1. For those who don't know, the Community Shield is the annual match between the Premier League Champions and FA Cup holders. The

Needless to say, Clint was a real cowboy. He used to ride rodeo and he farmed cattle. But he was also the pastor of a church of a hundred people in Calgary. He introduced his wife Christel and immediately the name rang a bell in my mind. It turned out that several months before we moved from the UK to Canada, I had been preparing a talk for a women's group in our church and stumbled across an article she had written about a particular godly woman called Sara Edwards. I never write on blogs, but this article was so good I typed a quick thank you. Then I noticed she lived in a place called High River in Alberta, and I wrote that I was moving to Alberta in 2008 with my wife and children. Some people might say it is coincidence that three and a half years later she walked into my church in the Rocky Mountains with her husband Clint who had contacted me out of the blue on social media. However, I call that another divine appointment.

I immediately got on well with Clint. Our minds thought alike to a great degree. We met a couple of times after this and he asked me to come on board at Calvary Grace Church of Calgary. After praying about it for a while and considering our options, it seemed good to do it and so we stayed. And several years later, as I write, we are still here. I currently serve as an Associate Pastor at Calvary Grace Church alongside fellow elders Clint, Paul Toews, Rob Snyder, Geoff Meadows and Josh Kary. They are all fine men. I preach and teach, regularly counsel church members, visit the sick, make decisions and give direction to the church with my fellow elders. I have a particular focus on, and responsibility for, building up men and growing healthy marriages. There is a tremendous need for this today. The Bible provides the instruction and pattern for what a man and a woman should be in marriage – the foundation of society

---

winner receives the big, silver-plated shield.

and a picture of Christ, the Bridegroom and His Bride, the Church.

Interestingly God has opened up doors for a wider ministry outside of my own church. So, although I came to Canada in obscurity, I travel to the UK, China, Africa, the USA and other parts of Canada to preach, give a testimony of God's grace through my life story, and teach seminars on manhood, womanhood and marriage. I've also co-authored a book on the subject, *The Grand Design* – written in tandem with my good friend, Professor Owen Strachan. Owen, like me, loves sports but loves God more, and he is a man of great courage whom I admire. He is one of those men who will stand by you in adversity. He has done this when others haven't, and this makes him a true friend.

If you had told me when I was a young man that I would go from being a football player to a football pundit to a gospel preacher, I would never have believed you. But actually, it is the greatest calling because preaching is the greatest need of the hour. To be tasked with proclaiming the truth of the Scriptures for the good of people and for God's glory is a weighty task, which I don't take lightly. But it's this truth that God's own Son, Jesus Christ, came to earth to preach when He said to a broken, sinning and suffering world,

> Come to me, all who labour and are heavy laden, and I will give you rest. Take my yoke upon you and learn from me, for I am gentle and humble in heart, and you will find rest for your souls (Matt. 11:28-29).

And that's what we all need; what you, the reader, needs. Rest. Rest from pain and sickness and all the maladies in your life and the world you see around you; and you need a kind of rest and peace and joy that will last more than a moment when everything goes right for a day or your team wins on a Saturday. That is a temporary kind of rest. But Jesus offers a rest that lasts forever. It's rest for the soul. And we will return to this in the final chapter.

11

A FAMILY PORTRAIT

Apart from the Lord God there is nothing more important to me than my family. We live in a day when family is not valued as the cornerstone of society and not considered necessary for the health and future of a culture and a country. Family is meant to provide love and security and a place to grow in strength and wisdom. Family is meant to give a sense of identity and belonging and community, as the different members endeavour to work together in harmony. Not that many years ago, parents used to remind sons and daughters that they were representing the family when they stepped out of the front door (as mine did before my first day at Bexley Grammar School) and that any misdemeanour brought shame upon the family not just the individual. So, true family engenders being centred on others. This is lost in an age of individualism where the home has lost its meaning and become a place to co-exist rather than co-operate.

Technology has made it so that dad, mum and two kids can be in the same house, yet with each having their own 'virtual' life, all on different devices, all in different corners of the building. Tragically, more than ever, families are divided, and we see the effects of that in a fatherless culture. These things

I have spoken of earlier in the book. Family is important in the Bible. God is called the Father and Jesus is called the Son. Many of us have been taught the Lord's prayer, 'Our Father in heaven, hallowed be your name...'. The biblical nuclear family is ordered, disciplined and harmonious, aimed at producing obedient children, who in turn become useful members of society and who are taught to love and honour God, the government and their parents. Christians are referred to as children of God, the Father. Husbands and wives in marriage portray a picture of Jesus, the Bridegroom and His Bride, the Church. And churches are called the family of God in which dwell spiritual brothers and sisters, fathers and mothers. All this is to say that family is very important in the Bible and at the most basic levels of human existence.

Although my family made sacrifices because of football, football was never worth more than them in my heart. They are my greatest trophies. So, here is a brief family portrait.

Amanda

My family begins with my wife, Amanda. She is my first love on this earth. We are a team of two equals and yet we are physically and functionally different. I take a lead as protector and provider, and she is my helper. This may sound old-fashioned, but it is very biblical and, apart from the past sixty years or so, was historical, traditional marriage teaching. Both the role of husband and wife require sacrifice for the other person, all for order and unity in the home.

Amanda worked outside the home in our early marriage but when our children were born she remained at home nurturing and teaching them. Nevertheless, we have kept our marriage a priority ahead of the children. Children don't make a family. A husband and wife are already a family. If you make children the bedrock and foundation of your marriage, what does your marriage stand on when the children leave home? That's why so many couples at that stage of life look at one another and see a stranger. This is because they've neglected to view their relationship as *holy* matrimony, with the need to tend to each other and grow together. Instead they have grown apart. A Christian marriage is built upon the foundation of Jesus Christ – and with husband and wife in a one-flesh union that is meant to portray God's love for the Church. The husband and wife are a family and children expand the family. Children who are raised with that kind of security feel more loved and flourish better. Amanda has fulfilled her role as my wife with great diligence.

She has also turned her hand to learning many things during our life together. She has worked with special-needs children and young adults. She has learned British Sign Language and volunteered her time at a centre for the deaf. She has learned pottery and studied art. She has also gained a certificate in biblical counselling. She teaches many women in our church and speaks on the family at Christian conferences for women.

The book of Proverbs gives a portrait of a godly wife and mother in chapter thirty-one. It says that 'her children rise up and call her blessed'. Amanda has been, and still is, a wonderful mother to Jake and Ava and they know it. She has cared for them well and her wisdom has equipped them for a God-honouring life in their own marriages. She has shown our son the character to look for in a good wife, and she has shown our daughter how to be that wife and mother. Now, as we pass thirty years of marriage, it is true that Amanda is my crown – my cherished companion and counsellor. We have experienced many trials and triumphs together and come through with our faith and marriage stronger. She is also a fine role model, friend and spiritual mother to many women in our church.

And she remains the source of warmth, softness, gentleness and compassion in our home and family. She is a good daughter, sister, aunt and friend. Amanda is many things to many people. But she is my wife and my one true love.

Jake

Our firstborn came into the world fighting for life in May 1993 and has exemplified that 'never say die' attitude throughout his twenty-six years so far. Having only one hand added pressure to Jake's childhood that many other children didn't have to experience. He endured years of people's strange looks, unkind words and clumsy comments. But he was a loving boy who, although he was strong and courageous, showed tender compassion as well. He was highly energetic: a risk taker who pushed boundaries, so he needed a firm hand and good guidance to channel his energies. He was, and still is, fiercely protective of his wife, mother and sister.

Jake was always popular at school and a keen sportsman. He played football, rugby and competed in athletics. In Canada he was the kicker for his high school American football team and captained the soccer team to win the regional title. But he excelled in martial arts from a young age. He even competed at an international level and represented Western Canada in the Kyokushin World Youth Championships in Tokyo at age seventeen.

Although a child may be brought up in a Christian home and taught about the faith, it doesn't guarantee he or she will own it for himself or herself. Jake was around seventeen years old when he became really convicted of his need of Jesus Christ as Lord and Saviour. From that moment he grew exponentially as a man. He graduated high school and then went to college where he gained a degree in Behavioral Science and, more importantly, met his wife-to-be, Christa. The moment we met her I said to Amanda, 'I think we have just seen our future daughter-in-law.' It was that obvious. In January 2016, they married at ages twenty-two and twenty-one years old in Christa's hometown of Estevan in Saskatchewan. It is a bittersweet moment when your children marry. You know it is good and right. But you also know things are changing and will never be the same again. Nevertheless, we gained a sweet and godly daughter in Christa, and it was my great pleasure to conduct the ceremony that day.

Jake has shown physical and moral courage in his life and he opened a martial arts gym called Dunamis (Greek for 'power') in the summer of 2017. The gym is a place where Jake teaches all ages with a focus on Muay Thai and boxing. The aim is fitness for all and for some a professional career in the sport. Christa, a gifted all-round sportswoman, works with him and they form a good partnership.

Jake has had a few professional Muay Thai fights in the past couple of years and continues to win and improve. His story is one that inspires many. It is a tale of perseverance in the face of adversity. In August 2019 he signed a contract for Las Vegas-based Muay Thai promoters, *Lion Fight*. That's apt I think because if I were to use one word to describe my son it would be this one: 'Lionheart'. Bravery marks him out and makes him a leader to be followed. But even more important than this is that he follows Jesus, whom the Bible calls – 'the Lion of the tribe of Judah' (Rev. 5:5). There is nothing more a father could want for his son than that, and no father could love and be more pleased with his son than me.

Ava

When Ava Eleanor arrived on the scene in June 1996, I didn't realize how differently I could feel about a daughter than a son.

Of course, I loved them both equally. But there is a different feel in the love a father has for his daughter: a sense of protection, which though it's there for a son, increases even more for a daughter. Whilst Jake was an action man from early on, Ava sat there for sixteen months taking everything in around her but deciding not to walk anywhere! However, she talked early and then she talked and talked and talked! In fact, whereas our son wore us out physically, our daughter exhausted us mentally. But as she grew, she combined a keen intellect with a love for music and a love for people. She had a sense of responsibility from a young age and showed a heart of compassion expressed in a desire to help others. From eleven years old she was even tutoring other children in her class and showing a desire to be a teacher and equipper of others.

Ava has always been family minded and loved her home and school life. She adjusted well to life in Canada and became an excellent student, singer and sportswoman – gaining her teaching qualification, singing in choirs and in church, playing all sports with distinction and representing Alberta at provincial level for team handball. For children in a Christian home who profess faith when they are adults it often is hard for them to discern when they became a Christian. But you are not born a Christian. You become a Christian at some point. I'm not exactly sure when it was for Ava, but I saw her really grow in her faith from the age of fifteen onwards. She has a lively faith that has shaped her desires and ambitions. She always wanted to be a wife and mother and make a home for her husband and children. She has a vision of the biblical family and great loyalty to family and friends. So even though she gained her degree in history and a teaching qualification, the home remains her priority.

She met Austin at the same college Jake met Christa. Actually, they all knew each other, and are still friends today and members of our church in Calgary. My antennae immediately went up when Ava started to mention Austin's name in conversation with increasing frequency. 'Oh no!' I thought, 'Here we go!' Then he asked to meet me at a café in town. Surprisingly – and to my great joy – his first question was not about Ava but about God and the Bible. I was encouraged because I knew that the man who would marry my daughter must be a man led by God first. Austin showed great teachability – something vital to anyone if they will do well. After a few weeks he asked to date Ava with a view to marriage and eventually they were married in May 2018.

As we gained a daughter with our lovely Christa, we gained a fine son in Austin, who works as a petroleum engineer technologist for an oil company in Calgary. Also, as a college-level volleyball player he keeps the sporting theme going in the family. I conducted the marriage ceremony again but my fellow pastor, Rob, had to do the introduction and opening words because I needed to walk in with Ava. That day I walked my daughter down the aisle and gave her away something inside my heart broke. It's a strange feeling. The little girl I held in my arms for so many years was now a woman on my arm. From this moment on, the man she would look to first was not her dad, it was now Austin. It was a good but painful reality. Nevertheless, Ava will always be her father's beloved, sweet, singing angel.

A man wants to leave a legacy in his life. If my wife and children are my legacy, then that is enough for me. I've had many roles in life as a footballer, pundit and pastor, but my first and most important role is as a Christian husband and father. And I have loved this role more than any other. My family is, as it were, my letter of recommendation for my leadership in the church. Because if you want to know how I will shepherd the family of God, look at my own family. I am a flawed man, not perfect by any means. But I have tried to follow God's Word for my marriage and children, let Him overcome my deficiencies and trusted Him with the brushstrokes of our family portrait.

12

A GREATER GLORY

There is a photograph that sits in my collection, which encapsulates what football means to so many. It was taken on the last day of the season in 1993 at St James' Park when we celebrated winning the First Division Championship and promotion to the Premier League. Team-mate, Robert Lee, and I are leading the team in a lap of honour, holding the trophy between us high and lifted up to the fans in the East Stand. Defender, Brian Kilcline, is pulling a Newcastle hat onto his head. Midfielder, Kevin Sheedy, walks on the green turf, head down as he drapes a Newcastle scarf around his neck. We all have scarves! English bobbies seem to be joining in the fun – no need to keep the peace today. Star striker, Andy Cole, stands tall as he strides across the turf in the background, hardly able to take in the electric atmosphere and the magnitude of the moment.

Behind us towards the top right of the photograph emerges the scoreboard with 'Champions' written across it. Below the scoreboard and providing the backdrop for the picture is a sea of fans that fills the Gallowgate End to overflowing – one person is even perched precariously on top of the Vauxhall Motors advertising board. But although the glint of the trophy that Lee and I hold catches the eye, there is a man dressed in a grey overcoat, cloth cap and tie who walks just off centre in the picture – and it is for him that the trophy shines most brightly.

His name is Stevie Charlton. He is sixty-two years old at the time and, after the players and manager, is perhaps the best-known face around the ground. He has followed the team home and away since he was five years old. He is there at every home game as we run out of the tunnel and onto the pitch. We shake hands, we give him a hug, our manager Kevin Keegan gives him a 'lucky' sweet. He used to work at St James' Park selling peanuts when he was younger. Newcastle is his passion. His life has been tough: he was an orphan staying at the Salvation Army accommodations, with no family of his own. Yet he was taken in and adopted by the Holmes family who own Holmes Bros. fruit stall in Newcastle. He grew up in that home and yet Newcastle United became his bigger family. Stevie represents the thousands of fans in the stadium and what their football club means to them. It's about a city, their team, a sense of dignity and belonging and the persevering hope of glory.

In all of us there is a desire for identity, a desire to belong and be accepted, and a desire to praise something glorious. We see echoes of this, particularly in football. Football fans find an identity in the team they support. They find pleasure in a sense of belonging and camaraderie. This feeling of acceptance comes simply because they support the same team. And their desire for praise of the big and beautiful and glorious is found in the players who become their heroes. And through their team, supporters can participate in something that takes them beyond the ordinary to a sense of victory in lives filled with many hardships and defeats.

Old Stevie Charlton died of heart failure in 2004 at age eighty-three, having suffered from Parkinson's disease for much of his last twenty years. Even that illness only stopped him attending a handful of matches. Stevie was called Newcastle United's 'Superfan'. He followed the team for nearly eighty years. It was said of him, 'Newcastle was his life.' This brings up the question: what is your life? What is the meaning and purpose of life? The common response is, 'Just live each day to the full and make the most of loved ones around you.' But that offers no lasting hope, purpose or pleasure. The mind-set says you're born, you live, and you die. That's it. So, eat drink and be merry. Get what you can out of it. That's selfish. And it is hopeless. I have mixed with some of the most wealthy and talented sportsmen of a generation and I've seen first-hand how none finds true satisfaction in that way of thinking. It has only led to futility, addiction, divorce and frustration time and again. Even the highs are only high for a moment. Then they crash back down to earth.

However, the Christian mind-set says, you're born, you live, you die, and yet you live. That's hope. You see, the Bible actually starts with God, not man. The first words read: 'In the beginning, God created the heavens and the earth' (Gen. 1:1). And then soon after it says: 'So God created man in his own image, in the image of God he created him; male and female he created them' (Gen. 1:27). And then: 'And God saw everything that he had made and behold, it was very good' (Gen. 1:31).

God is the creator and God is good, and this is expressed in the fact that in the beginning all He creates is good. Therefore, the Bible's view of man is that he is of great worth. He is created in God's image with the ability to know Him and obey Him. Man is not, as some would say, an accident of nature, chemical explosions or amoebic evolution. This is hopeful and full of dignity. It should give you a sense of purpose for a start. You and I were made by God and for God, in order to obey and represent God in some way. This means we are accountable to God. And that is a good and safe thing.

God's goodness and generosity is shown in the fact that He makes a beautiful place for the man and woman – Eden. And He gives them everything for their enjoyment and needs. He gives them food and fruit and says they can eat from any tree except one. But they took the forbidden fruit in the Garden of Eden. And ever since Adam and Eve sinned by disobeying God, all men and women 'have sinned and fall short of the glory of God' (Rom. 3:23). Our sin is our selfish heart that wants to do our own thing and not what God commands. We love ourselves more than God. Our sin is the reason for suffering, sickness and death. Our sin is the reason for divorce and war, rape and child abuse, poverty and famine and the fractured world in which we live. Furthermore, the Bible tells us that sin is not just a sickness; man is not a victim, he is a rebel against God and His authority over us as those to whom He gives life. To sum it all up: The Bible says that God is a good and generous Creator and man has sinned against Him. The Bible also says that this means God must judge sin because God is holy and good. So, Adam and Eve were banished from the Garden.

If you see God and sin like this you see why the Bible says, 'the wages of sin are death' (Rom. 6:23). This a problem which humanity throughout history has not been able to solve no matter how many attempts we make. Everybody dies. But the enduring judgement is not just physical, it is spiritual. To die without your sins being dealt with means to remain under God's judgement for eternity in hell. That is why the gospel is the good news about God taking the initiative to love and reconcile sinful people to Himself. How? Remember the banner you see at so many World Cups and major sporting events? 'God so loved the world that he gave his only Son, that whoever believes in him should not perish but have eternal life' (John 3:16).

This is why we traditionally celebrate Christmas. It's about that moment when God became a man in Jesus Christ. Because we can't save ourselves, we need a Saviour. The Gospel of Matthew puts it like this: 'And you shall call his name Jesus for he will save his people from their sins' (Matt. 1:21). Jesus saves people by living the perfect life that we can never achieve and by taking the punishment on the cross that we deserve. And that's what Christians remember at Easter: what Jesus did on the cross. Think of it like this: Jesus is the perfect substitute who steps onto the field for us, rescues us from defeat, and secures victory. Jesus frees us from guilt and condemnation. And when He rose from the dead three days after the cross, He promised to return and He promised an eternal future in heaven with no more sin, suffering or sorrow. The last book of the Bible confirms this: 'He will wipe away every tear from their eyes, and death shall be no more, neither shall there be mourning, nor crying, nor pain anymore, for the former things have passed away' (Rev. 21:4).

You might think this is crazy, untrue or delusional, but this is the testimony of the Bible. It is the testimony of historic Christianity. It is the testimony of millions of Christians in churches worldwide today and throughout the ages. And it logically explains the reason why we exist, the reason why we die and the reason for real hope. Christianity is the only religion that satisfactorily deals with the problem of our reconciliation to God and to each other, because it is the only religion where God comes down as a man to freely save mankind. We don't deserve it or earn it, He just gives it. This is called *grace*. All you need to do is turn from your sins. This is called *repentance*. And then receive this gift and trust in Jesus for forgiveness and new life. This is called *faith*.

Once you know that God made you and you were made for Him; once you know that sin is the root problem in your life;

and once you know what the solution to the problem is – the good news about Jesus who came to save sinners through His life, death and resurrection – and once you know what you need to do – repent and believe in Him – then your world begins to make sense.

Throughout this book I have touched on some deep issues: life, death, sin, suffering, success, failure, marriage, family, friendship, teamwork, identity, belonging and hope. But all these words find their meaning in Jesus Christ: Jesus is the one who offers eternal *life* and victory over *death, sin* and *suffering.* Following Jesus through many hardships is the true way to *success* and sustains us in the *failures* we experience in this life. Becoming a Christian doesn't immunize you against suffering, but being a Christian sustains you through suffering, because there is hope beyond the pain. In Jesus we find the true meaning of *marriage.* He is the Bridegroom who came to die for His Bride, the Church. Jesus, the Son of God, brings those who trust in Him into the *family* of God as children of God the Father, so that even those with broken families on earth can know a perfect Father in heaven and a spiritual family of brothers and sisters in the church. Jesus is the perfect *friend* who will never let you down and who will be with you in harness as a *team* forever. Jesus gives a person true *identity, belonging* and *hope* for a better life to come, which helps us persevere in this life today.

So this book, my twelve stones is, as I said from the start, a memorial – a story of an ordinary man, which takes you all the way from the pitch to the pulpit. But I hope that you now see it is ultimately a memorial of God's amazing grace. I hope that you, the reader, see that there is more to life than football, fame and fortune. There is another glory for you to see – a greater glory. It is the greatest glory. It is the glory of God in the face of Jesus Christ. It is the beauty that is found in the love of God through the Son of God who died and rose so you may live, trusting Him for salvation and spending your life in His service. Then you will know that you live for something that can never be taken away.

Think of that photograph and the Newcastle United victory lap and old Stevie Charlton. As a Christian, when you have run the race of life, the crowds will cheer as you run a victory lap in heaven, but the focus will not be on you or a trophy, but on Jesus Christ. Because He is the one who gives victory in the arena. And until that day you will live on the promise that, 'they who wait for the LORD shall renew their strength; they shall mount up with wings like eagles; they shall run and not be weary; they shall walk and not faint' (Isa. 40:31).

Football is a great game: the best in my opinion. But if you look to football or anything else for ultimate purpose, it won't last, it won't satisfy, and it won't eventually save you. Football is great. But Jesus is greater.

***

I wake up. It's 6 am on Sunday morning. Amanda is still sleeping. I make coffee, go to my study and open my Bible at the passage I will preach this morning in church. I look out of the window across the forest of trees that line the immediate horizon. I turn my gaze towards the majestic Rocky Mountains to the West. The moon is still faintly in view as the orange glow of the sunrise shines on snowy peaks. All of creation belongs to God and is His handiwork. I pray. I think of the church members who will be there today and the many struggles they have. I think of those who are not Christian and who may come along this morning. Breakfast. Shower. Suit on. We drive to Calvary Grace Church. Snow is on the ground.

Henry is on the door welcoming people today. A friendly face and a firm handshake await visitors. 'Hello, Pastor Gavin and Amanda' says Grace as we enter the church. There's Leslie, taking his coat off and sitting down in the foyer. He's been unwell. Looks better today though. Little John comes up to me and tugs at my jacket. 'Arsenal are better than Chelsea' says the seven-year-old, as he points to the Gunners badge on his top. Two people ask to see me afterwards for some counsel. The music team practises as I enter the sanctuary. Pews are filling. People are filing in. That's a new face over there. Amanda makes a mental note to go over and say hello after the service. I go into the Pastors' room at the front of the church.

Clint, Rob, Geoff, Paul and Josh come in one by one. This is the leadership team. Good men. We pray. We go to our seats. The service begins. The opening Bible reading calls everyone together. The first hymn. I look along my pew. Amanda, Jake, Christa, Ava and Austin stand side by side: linked together by love, always together in Christ. Christa is pregnant, her belly is full of life. A next generation of Peacocks is about to be born. How far we have come from the UK to here. A foretaste of heaven as all of us sing. My sermon text is read out. A few butterflies in the stomach. Like match day almost. But today the stakes are higher. People's souls matter more than victory on the football field. A quick prayer. I get up from my seat and begin to make my way to the pulpit. All my senses are heightened. What a journey! From pitch to pulpit. The multitudes of fans in the stadium and the millions of viewers on TV are gone. And I stand in front of a congregation of 200, Bible open, sermon in front of me. I look out at the faces. Silence. This is my family. In the pain and pleasures of their lives they need to hear what the Bible says about Jesus. Eternal things are at stake. In a world where we don't know what tomorrow will bring, He is the only one who can save us and sustain us and comfort us. I remember the words of John the Baptist: 'He must increase, but I must decrease.'

I open my mouth…and preach the Word.

In honour of my loving parents.

For you I am ever grateful.

ACKNOWLEDGEMENTS

Reflecting upon one's life after fifty years is quite the task. Putting it all down in writing, structuring it in book form and getting it ready for publishing is another challenge altogether. But before all this takes place there is always someone who gives you that nudge to get started. So, I wish to thank Willie Mackenzie who, several years back, gave me that encouraging word to begin this project. In fact, the whole Christian Focus team has done a stellar job as usual, with special mention to Rosanna Burton, Margaret Roberts, Kate Mackenzie, Peter Matthess and James Amour – plus Anna Michalska for use of her wonderful photography work.

Thank you, also, Stephen Greenhalgh and Anne Norrie for your keen editorial eyes as you diligently scanned the manuscript for hours. It was a pleasure to work with you both.

There are friends in life upon whom you can lean in any circumstance. So, it is appropriate that I make mention of Graham Daniels and Lance Hardy who took the time in their busy lives to read this text when it was in its infancy and gave me both encouragement and constructive feedback. One man in particular, who has been a big influence in my writing career, is Owen Strachan. Owen, you have given me wings to fly as an author – through the books we have written together and the many articles of mine that you have edited and platformed. Moreover, you are a true brother and a man of courageous conviction, of which there are too few. I also think we would have made a good partnership in midfield together!

Whether I write about being on the football field or in the pundit's chair this book is flavoured with the beautiful game and those involved. I have been so blessed to make many many friends and acquaintances in the context of this thrilling sport of beauty and power. Therefore, my gratitude goes out to all of my managers and team-mates, and the thousands and thousands of fans who pay their hard-earned money to watch and who make the game what it is.

To my wife, Amanda, my greatest helper in all things: you have done it again – even as we discussed aspects of this book before and after pen was put to page. Your sharp insights and editorial eye were invaluable. For you I am thankful every day.

Finally, my thanks go to my God and heavenly Father who gives every breath we breathe, who granted me the ability to kick a piece of leather around a field quite well, who enabled me to articulate this on a TV screen or radio airwaves and who allowed me the honour of serving as a leader in the church. Thanks be to Him who gave me this wonderful life on earth and eternal life in the Lord Jesus Christ: the one who does all things well (Mark 7:37).

Also available from Christian Focus publications...

BY JOHN W. KEDDIE

RUNNING THE RACE

ERIC LIDDELL

OLYMPIC CHAMPION & MISSIONARY

RUNNING THE RACE

ERIC LIDDELL – OLYMPIC CHAMPION
AND MISSIONARY

JOHN W. KEDDIE

The name Eric Liddell is a familiar one to many, having gained much fame through the film *Chariots of Fire*. A Christian athlete and missionary, his passion for his Saviour could be seen throughout his life. From university days to internment at Weihsien POW Camp, John Keddie's biography brings together a specialist understanding of both Liddell's faith and sporting achievements to provide an engaging account of this normal man's extraordinary life.

Former athlete and churchman John Keddie brings both sporting expertise and spiritual insight to this lucid and meticulous biography of the great Eric Liddell.

Sally Magnusson
Broadcaster (Reporting Scotland, Songs of Praise) & Author of several books, including *The Flying Scotsman: The Eric Liddell Story*

It is abundantly clear from these pages that the driving force in Liddell's life was love for his Lord and Saviour Jesus Christ and that he lived by the wisdom of Ecclesiastes 9:10: 'Whatever your hand finds to do, do it with all your might.' This is an inspiring and challenging account of the life of a truly inter–continental hero and will be enjoyed by the sporting enthusiast and Christian alike.

Euan Murray
Former Scottish Rugby Union Player

ISBN 978-1-5271-0531-7

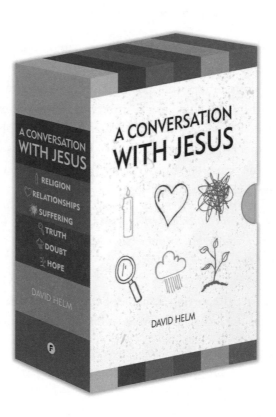

A CONVERSATION WITH JESUS

DAVID HELM

Six people – and their conversations with Jesus in the verses of John's Gospel – are examined in this inspiring, thoughtful slip-cased collection on Christian belief and the meaning behind Jesus' words. Each volume focuses on a specific theme, and is written in direct, simple language designed to help Christians find guidance in their lives across a range of topics, including:

- **Truth** and Jesus' words with Pontius Pilate during His trial
- **Suffering**, and the conversation with the lame man healed by the pool of Bethesda
- **Religion** with Nicodemus the Pharisee
- **Hope** and His conversations with Mary Magdalene
- The nature and consequences of **Doubt**, with Thomas the Apostle
- The nature of **Relationships**, from Jesus' conversation with the woman at the well

The church in western society has never had a greater need for books like this to give to inquirers who are open to considering what real Christianity looks like. These six short studies are gems of lucidity. Use them!

Tim Keller
Redeemer City to City

ISBN 978-1-5271-0323-8

JOE
BARNARD

THE
WAY
FORWARD

**A ROADMAP
OF SPIRITUAL GROWTH
FOR MEN IN THE 21ST CENTURY**

THE WAY FORWARD

A ROAD MAP OF SPIRITUAL GROWTH
FOR MEN IN THE 21ST CENTURY

JOE BARNARD

A lot of Christian men feel stuck. They have a sincere desire to grow but feel confused about what to do next. *The Way Forward* is a road-map for men who want to cut through the noise and distraction of the 21st century and take definite steps toward spiritual maturity. This book follows the simple format of problem, solution, and plan. Men who read it will walk away with both a clear diagnosis for why they feel stuck and a practical action plan for moving forward.

Joe Barnard has a passion to help young Christian men become more spiritually fit and effective in their families and communities. His book has much insight and a lot of practical help toward that goal. What he desires is more potent servants of Christ, and anyone who aspires to be such a servant will profit much from reading his book.

David Lyle Jeffrey
Distinguished Senior Fellow, Baylor Institute for Studies in
Religion & Emeritus Distinguished Professor of Literature and the
Humanities, Baylor University, Waco, Texas

ISBN 978-1-5271-0467-9

Christian Focus Publications

Our mission statement –

STAYING FAITHFUL
In dependence upon God we seek to impact the world through literature faithful to His infallible Word, the Bible. Our aim is to ensure that the Lord Jesus Christ is presented as the only hope to obtain forgiveness of sin, live a useful life and look forward to heaven with Him.

Our books are published in four imprints:

CHRISTIAN FOCUS

Popular works including biographies, commentaries, basic doctrine and Christian living.

CHRISTIAN HERITAGE

Books representing some of the best material from the rich heritage of the church.

MENTOR

Books written at a level suitable for Bible College and seminary students, pastors, and other serious readers. The imprint includes commentaries, doctrinal studies, examination of current issues and church history.

CF4•K

Children's books for quality Bible teaching and for all age groups: Sunday school curriculum, puzzle and activity books; personal and family devotional titles, biographies and inspirational stories – because you are never too young to know Jesus!

Christian Focus Publications Ltd,
Geanies House, Fearn, Ross-shire,
IV20 1TW, Scotland, United Kingdom.
www.christianfocus.com